Training Manual
for
Industrial Training Institutes (ITIs)

(As on 1st January 2014)

Part 1

THIRD EDITION

Training Manual
for
Industrial Training Institutes (ITIs)

(As on 1st January 2014)

Part 1

THIRD EDITION

Directorate General of Employment and Training
Ministry of Labour
Government of India
New Delhi

McGraw Hill Education (India) Private Limited
NEW DELHI

McGraw Hill Education Offices
New Delhi New York St Louis San Francisco Auckland Bogotá Caracas
Kuala Lumpur Lisbon London Madrid Mexico City Milan Montreal
San Juan Santiago Singapore Sydney Tokyo Toronto

McGraw Hill Education (India) Private Limited

Published by McGraw Hill Education (India) Private Limited
P-24, Green Park Extension, New Delhi 110 016

Training Manual for Industrial Training Institutes (ITIs) Part 1

ISBN-13: 978-9-35-134157-4
ISBN-10: 9-35-134157-7

Vice President and Managing Director: *Ajay Shukla*

Head—Higher Education Publishing and Marketing: *Vibha Mahajan*
Senior Publishing Manager—SEM & Tech Ed.: *Shalini Jha*
Senior Media Developer: *Baldev Raj*
Manager—Production Systems: *Satinder S Baveja*
Assistant Manager—Editorial Services: *Sohini Mukherjee*

Assistant General Manager—Higher Ed.: *Vijay Sarathi*
Senior Product Specialist—SEM & Tech Ed.: *Tina Jajoriya*
General Manager—Production: *Rajender P Ghansela*
Manager— Production: *Reji Kumar*

Typeset at The Composers, 260, C.A. Apt., Paschim Vihar, New Delhi 110 063 and printed at
Sanat Printers, 312, EPIP, HSIDC, Kundli, Sonepat, Haryana

Cover Printer: Sanat Printers

Preface to the Third Edition

This Training Manual is a comprehensive guide for all relevant information pertaining to the Craftsmen Training Scheme of the Government of India, Ministry of Labour, being implemented in Industrial Training Institutes all over the country. It has been divided into two parts. **Part I** contains information on the Organisation Structure, Administration of Industrial Institutes, Manpower Requirements, All India Skills Competition under the Craftsmen Training Scheme and Prescribed Standards. Chapter 1 covers the details of the National Vocational Training System. Chapter 2 presents the Craftsmen Training Scheme (CTS). Chapter 3 describes Manpower Requirement, Role and Responsibilities of Industrial Training Institutes. Chapter 4 gives details of the All India Trade Test Procedure for the Craftsmen Training Scheme Under the Aegis of NCVT. Finally, Appendices I to XXIII deal with various topics related to CTS and present sample certificates awarded to trainees at the end of their courses. **Part II**, which is in the process of finalisation at present, contains the Affiliation Procedure and Accreditation Criteria for Government and Private Industrial Training Institutes seeking NCVT affiliation.

Detailed information supplementing the text contained in the above parts, such as various prescribed proformae, statistical returns, procedures, etc., has been included in the relevant appendices and annexures to the manual.

The Training Manual is an attempt to provide a transparent system to the end users of the Craftsmen Training Scheme. Any training scheme, being non-static in nature, requires continuous review and updating of policies, procedures, rules, standards, etc., so that the socio-economic changes, technical advancements and training needs of user industries are appropriately taken care of. The last revision of this manual was done in 2002. After that the National Council for Vocational Training (NCVT) has made a number of recommendations and necessary orders for the implementation of prescribed norms that were issued from time to time. The training manual has been revised to incorporate these orders at the appropriate places.

It may, however, be clarified that this manual is not a legal document, but is made only to serve the users for smooth implementation of the norms prescribed by NCVT. For any clarification, the original office orders relating to that recommendation may be referred to.

It is hoped that the State Directorates dealing with Craftsmen Training, Principals and Staff of ITIs, trainees and all those concerned with the implementation of the Craftsmen Training Scheme would continue to find this manual a very useful reference.

DGE&T
Ministry of Labour
New Delhi

Preface to the Second Edition

This Training Manual is a comprehensive guide for all relevant information pertaining to the Craftsmen Training Scheme of the Government of India, Ministry of Labour, being implemented in Industrial Training Institutes/Centres all over the country. It has been divided into five parts, viz., (i) Organisation, (ii) Administration of Industrial Training Institutes, (iii) Institute Staff, (iv) General Information, and (v) Prescribed Standards.

Detailed information supplementing the text contained in the above parts, such as various prescribed proformae, statistical returns, procedures, etc., has been included in the relevant appendices and annexures to the manual.

The Training Manual is an attempt to provide a transparent system to the end users of Craftsmen Training Scheme. Any training scheme, being non-static in nature, requires continuous review and updating of policies, procedures, rules, standards, etc., so that the socio-economic changes, technical advancements and training needs of user industries are appropriately taken care of. The last revision of this manual was done in 1995. After that the National Council for Vocational Training (NCVT) has made a number of recommendations and necessary orders for the implementation of prescribed norms that were issued from time to time. The training manual has been revised to incorporate these orders at the appropriate places.

It may, however, be clarified that this manual is not a legal document, but is made only to serve the users for smooth implementation of the norms prescribed by NCVT. For any clarification, the original office orders relating to that recommendation may be referred to.

It is hoped that the State Directorates dealing with Craftsmen Training, Principals and Staff of ITIs/ITCs, trainees and all those concerned with the implementation of the Craftsmen Training Scheme would continue to find this manual a very useful reference.

DGE&T
Ministry of Labour
New Delhi

Preface to the First Edition

This Training Manual is a comprehensive guide for all relevant information pertaining to the Craftsmen Training Scheme of the Government of India, Ministry of Labour, being implemented in Industrial Training Institutes/Centres all over the country. It has been divided into five parts, viz., (i) Organisation, (ii) Administration of Industrial Training Institutes, (iii) Institute Staff, (iv) General Information, and (v) Prescribed Standards.

Detailed information supplementing the text contained in the above parts, such as various prescribed proformae, statistical returns, procedures, etc., has been included in the relevant appendices and annexures to the manual.

Any training scheme, being non-static in nature, requires continuous review and updating of policies, procedures, rules, standards, etc., so that the socio-economic changes, technical advancements and training needs of user industries are appropriately taken care of. It is suggested that the manual may always be read along with the instructions/orders issued from time to time so that information is correct and up-to-date.

It is hoped that the State Directorates dealing with Craftsmen Training, Principals and Staff of ITIs/ITCs, trainees and all those concerned with the implementation of the Craftsmen Training Scheme would continue to find this manual a very useful reference.

DGE&T
Ministry of Labour
New Delhi

Preface to the First Edition

This Training Manual is a comprehensive guide for all relevant information pertaining to the Craftsmen Training Scheme of the Government of India, Ministry of Labour, being implemented in Industrial Training Institutes/Centres all over the country. It has been divided into five parts viz., (i) Organisation, (ii) Administration of Industrial Training Institutes, (iii) Institute Staff, (iv) General Information and (v) Prescribed Standards.

Detailed information supplementing the text contained in the above parts such as various prescribed proformae, statistical returns, procedures, etc. has been included in the relevant appendices and annexures to the manual.

Any training scheme, being non-static in nature, requires continuous review and updating of policies, procedures, rules, standards, etc., so that the socio-economic changes, technical advancements and training needs of user industries are appropriately taken care of. It is suggested that the manual may always be read along with the instructions/orders issued from time to time so that information is correct and up-to-date.

It is hoped that the State Directorates dealing with Craftsmen Training, Principals and Staff of ITIs/ITCs, trainees and all those concerned with the implementation of the Craftsmen Training Scheme would continue to find this manual a very useful reference.

DGE&T
Ministry of Labour
New Delhi

Table of Content

Note from Publisher

Part II, which is under finalisation with DGE&T, contains. Affiliation Procedure and Accreditation Criteria for Government and Private Industrial Training Institutes seeking NCVT Affiliation. For any urgent requirement, please contact the Ministry of Labour, Directorate General of Employment and Training or visit their web site at http://dget.gov.in

PART I

Chapter 1

National Vocational Training System

1.1 NATIONAL POLICY ON SKILL DEVELOPMENT

The National Policy on Skill Development was approved by the Union Cabinet on 23 February, 2009. The policy is a guiding document for implementation of various skill-development programmes in the country. The objective is to create a workforce empowered with improved skills, knowledge and internationally recognised qualifications, which would enable them to gain access to decent employment and ensure India's competence in the dynamic global labour market.

The salient features of the policy are the following:

(i) Generating a demand-driven system guided by labour-market signals, in order to reduce skill mismatch
(ii) Expansion of outreach using established as well as innovative approaches
(iii) Setting up of the National Vocational Qualifications Framework, which will inter-alia include opportunities for horizontal and vertical mobility between general and technical education, and recognition and certification of competencies irrespective of mode of learning
(iv) Having a system to deliver 'competencies' in line with nationally and internationally recognised standards
(v) Focus on new emerging occupations
(vi) Focus on pre-employment training and lifelong learning
(vii) Equity consideration—adequate participation of women, disabled persons and disadvantaged groups including the economically backward and minorities—enhancing the workforce access to training; improving employability and increasing employment opportunities
(viii) Stress on research, planning and monitoring
(ix) Involvement of social partners—responsibility of management and financing of the system would be shared by all stakeholders and provide greater space for public-private partnership
(x) Promoting excellence
(xi) Use of modern training technologies including distance learning, e-learning, web-based learning, etc.
(xii) Skill upgradation of trainers, and their quality assurance and improvement of status

1.2 THE MISSION STATEMENT, AIMS AND OBJECTIVES

Mission The policy envisions the establishment of a National Skill Development Initiative with the following mission:

The National Skill Development Initiative will empower all individuals through improved skills, knowledge, and nationally and internationally recognised qualifications, which would enable the people to gain access to decent employment and ensure India's competence in the global market.

Aims The aim of skill development in the country is to achieve rapid and inclusive growth through

(i) Enhancing individuals' employability (wage/self-employment) and ability to adapt to changing technologies and labour-market demands
(ii) Improving productivity and living standards of the people
(iii) Strengthening competitiveness of the country
(iv) Attracting investment in skill development

Objectives of National Policy on Skill Development

The objectives of the National Policy on Skill Development are the following:

(i) Create opportunities for all, especially youth, women and disadvantaged groups, to acquire skills throughout life
(ii) Promote commitment by all stakeholders to own skill-development initiatives
(iii) Develop a high-quality skilled workforce/entrepreneurship relevant to current and emerging employment market needs
(iv) Enable the establishment of flexible delivery mechanisms that respond to the characteristics of a wide range of needs of stakeholders
(v) Enable effective coordination between different ministries, the centre and the states and public and private providers

Target set by National Policy on Skill Development (NPSD)

Skill development of 500 million persons by 2022 by involving all stakeholders through concerned ministers and departments

Scope of the National Policy on Skill Development

The coverage of the National Policy on Skill Development includes the following:

(i) Institution-based skill development including government and private ITIs/vocational schools/technical schools/polytechnics/professional colleges, etc.
(ii) Learning initiatives of sectoral skill development organised by different ministries/departments
(iii) Formal and informal apprenticeships and other types of training by enterprises
(iv) Training for self-employment/entrepreneurial development
(v) Adult learning, retraining of retired or retiring employees and lifelong learning
(vi) Non-formal training including training by civil society organisations
(vii) E-learning, web-based learning and distance learning

1.3 NATIONAL COUNCIL FOR VOCATIONAL TRAINING (NCVT)

The National Council for Vocational Training, an advisory body, was set up by the Government of India in 1956 (the then National Council of Training in Vocational Trades—NCTVT). The Council has been entrusted with the responsibilities of prescribing standards and curricula for craftsmen training, advising the Government of India on the overall policy and programmes, conducting All India Trade Tests and awarding National Trade Certificates.

1.4 ORGANISATIONAL SET-UP OF NCVT

Resolution In pursuance of the recommendation of the All India Council for Technical Education, the Government of India in the Ministry of Labour Resolution No. RTA-428(5)/dated 22 May, 1951, appointed a committee called the National Trade Certification Investigation Committee with instructions to prepare a scheme for the establishment of an All India Trades Board which would award certificates of proficiency to craftsmen in various engineering and building trades. The report of this committee and also the recommendation of the Training and Employment Services Organisation Committee (known as the Shiva Rao Committee) was considered by the Government of India. The Government agreed with both the committees that there was a need for setting up a central agency for coordinating the training programmes in the country, bringing about uniformity of standards and awarding certificates of proficiency in craftsmanship on an all-India basis. Such a step would be in the interest of both the industry and the workers in as much as it will ensure that the holders of National Certificates possess a minimum recognised degree of skill. In addition, it would facilitate mobility of tradesmen in search of better employment.

The Government of India also decided to transfer the administration of the training organisation under the Directorate General of Resettlement and Employment to the control of the State Government concerned, retaining for themselves the functions of co-ordinating craftsmen training and laying down the training policy. This decision has further accentuated the need for a central agency for assisting or advising the Central Government in the discharge of their responsibilities regarding Craftsmen Training. It has accordingly been decided, in consultation with the State governments and other concerned parties, to set up a National Council for Vocational Training (Accordingly, with a view to ensure and maintain uniformity in the standards of training all over the country, the National Council for Vocational Training, an advisory body, was set up by the Government of India in the year 1956. The Council has been entrusted with the responsibilities of prescribing standards and curricula for Craftsmen Training, advising the Government of India on the overall policy and programmes, conducting All India Trade Tests and awarding National Trade Certificates. The National Council is chaired by the Minister of Labour, with members representing Central and State Government departments, employers' and workers' organisations, professional and learned bodies, All India Council for Technical Education, Scheduled castes and Scheduled tribes, All India Women's Organisation, etc.). The State Council for Vocational Training at the State level and the Trade Committees have been established to assist the National Council.

The structure of the National Council for Vocational Training is given below:

Name The name of the Council shall be National Council for Vocational Training (NCVT).

Headquarters The headquarters of the Council shall be in New Delhi.

Objectives The Council shall function as a central agency to advise the Government of India in framing the training policy and coordinating vocational training throughout India.

Function The functions of the Council shall be to

(i) Establish and award National Trade Certificates in engineering, building, textile and leather trades and such other trades as may be brought within its scope by the Government of India
(ii) Prescribe standards in respect of syllabi, equipment, and scale of space, duration of courses and methods of training
(iii) Arrange trade tests in various trade courses and lay down standards of proficiency required for a pass in the trade test leading to the award of National Trade Certificate
(iv) Arrange for ad-hoc or periodical inspections of training institutions in the country to ensure that the standards prescribed by the Council are being followed
(v) Recognise training institutions run by government or by private agencies for purposes of the grant of National Trade Certificates and lay down conditions for such recognition
(vi) Co-opt, if necessary, any person or persons to advise the Council in connection with its work
(vii) Prescribe qualifications for the technical staff of training institutions
(viii) Prescribe the standards and conditions of eligibility for the award of National Trade Certificates
(ix) Generally control the conditions for the award of National Trade Certificates
(x) Recommend the provision of additional training facilities, wherever necessary, and render such assistance in the setting up of additional training institutions or in the Organisation of additional training programmes as may be possible
(xi) Advise the central government regarding distribution to state governments of the contribution of the Government of India towards expenditure on the Craftsmen Training Scheme
(xii) Perform such other functions as may be entrusted to it by the Government of India
(xiii) Perform such functions as are assigned by or under the Apprentices Act, 1961

1.5 COMPOSITION OF THE COUNCIL (AS PER RESOLUTION DATED 21/24 AUGUST, 1956)

The Council has been constituted by the Government of India and consists of the following members:

(i) Chairperson Union Minister of Labour/State Minister of Labour and Employment
(ii) Secretary to the Government of India, Ministry of Labour and Employment
(iii) Director General of Employment and Training, and one representative each of
  (a) Ministry of Transport and Shipping
  (b) Ministry of Communications
  (c) Ministry of Tourism and Civil Aviation
  (d) Department of Iron and Steel in the Ministry of Steel Mines and Metals
  (e) Small Scale Industries Organisations, Ministry of Industrial Development and Cooperative Affairs
  (f) Large and Medium Scale Industries Organisations, Ministry of Industrial Development and Cooperative Affairs
  (g) Public Sector Projects
  (h) Controller of Printing (Department of Printing and Stationery) in the Ministry of Works, Housing and Supply

(i) Central Public Work Department
(j) Ministry of Defence
(k) Ministry of Finance
(l) Ministry of Education
(m) Ministry of Railways
(n) Ministry of Irrigation and Power
(o) Department of Cooperation, Ministry of Food, Agriculture, Development and Cooperation
(p) Planning Commission
(q) Department of Atomic Energy
(r) Textile Commissioner to the Government of India or his/her representative in the Ministry of Commerce
(s) Directorate General of Technical Development in the Ministry of Industrial Development and Cooperative Affairs

The representatives will, as far as possible, be technical officers.

(iv) One representative from each state government and Union Territory of Delhi, Arunachal Pradesh, Manipur, Chandigarh, Goa, Daman and Diu and Pondicherry, Mizoram, and Dadra and Nagar Haveli
(v) Director General, Factory Advice Service and Labour Institute, Mumbai
(vi) Five representatives of employers' organizations nominated by the Government of India in consultation with the employers' organisations
(vii) Five representatives of workers' organisations nominated by the Government of India in consultation with the workers' organisations
(viii) Five representatives of professional and learned bodies nominated by the Government of India
(ix) One representative of the All India Council for Technical Education nominated by that Council
(x) Two experts appointed by the Government of India
(xi) One representative each of the scheduled castes and scheduled tribes
(xii) Director of Employment Exchanges (DGE&T), Ministry of Labour & Employment and Rehabilitation
(xiii) Member Secretary—Director of Training (DGE&T), Ministry of Labour & Employment and Rehabilitation
(xiv) One representative of an all-India women's organisation

1.6(A) COMPOSITION OF COUNCIL (w.e.f. 4 DECEMBER, 2010)

The Council shall be constituted by the Government of India and shall consist of the following members:

(i) Chairperson Union Minister for Labour and Employment/Minister of State for Labour and Employment (IC)
(ii) Vice Chairman—State Minister for Labour and Employment
(iii) Secretary to the Government of India, Ministry of Labour
(iv) Director General of Employment and Training/Joint Secretary, Ministry of Labour and Employment
(v) Financial Advisor Ministry of Labour and Employment
(vi) Deputy Director General (Training)

(vii) Deputy Director General (Apprenticeship Training) and one representative from each of the following:
   (a) Department of Technical Education, Ministry of Human Resource Development
   (b) Ministry of Textiles
   (c) Ministry of Communication and Information and Technology/Department of Information Technology
   (d) Ministry of Micro, Small and Medium Enterprises

The representatives will, as far as possible, be technical officers.

(viii) One representative each from state governments and union territory administrations (State Directors dealing with Craftsmen Training Scheme) of Andhra Pradesh, Assam, Chhattisgarh, Gujarat, Himachal Pradesh, Madhya Pradesh, Maharashtra, Karnataka, Kerala, Orissa, Punjab, Rajasthan, Tamil Nadu, Uttar Pradesh, West Bengal, Jammu and Kashmir, Haryana, Bihar, Delhi and Nagaland
(ix) Three representatives of employers' organisations nominated by the Government of India
(x) Three representatives of workers' organisations nominated by the Government of India
(xi) Five representatives of professional and learned bodies nominated by the Government of India
(xii) One representative of the All India Council for Technical Education nominated by the Government of India
(xiii) Five experts nominated by the Government of India
(xiv) One representative each of the scheduled castes and scheduled tribes nominated by the Government of India
(xv) One representative of a women's organisation nominated by the Government of India
(xvi) Member Secretary—Director of Training (DGE&T), Ministry of Labour and Employment

1.6(B) COMPOSITION OF COUNCIL (w.e.f. 1ST OCTOBER, 2013)

(a) Union Minister for Labour & Employment	Chairman
(b) Minister of State for Labour & Employment	Vice Chairman
(c) Secretary, Labour & Employment	Member
(d) Director General of Employment & Training	Member
(e) One representative each of:	
(i) Ministry of Micro, Small & Medium Enterprises	Member
(ii) Ministry of Textiles	Member
(iii) Department of Chemicals & Petro Chemicals	Member
(f) One representative each from State of:	
(i) Uttar Pradesh	Member
(ii) Bihar	Member
(iii) Maharashtra	Member
(iv) Rajasthan	Member
(v) Andhra Pradesh	Member
(vi) Tripura	Member
(vii) UT of Chandigarh	Member
(g) One representative of All India Council for Technical Education	Member
(h) Two representatives of Employers	Member
(i) Two representatives of Workers Organizations	Member
(j) Five experts to be nominated	Member
(k) Dy. Director General (Training), DGE&T	Member Secretary

1.7 TERMS OF OFFICE OF MEMBERS

The terms of office of all non-official members of the Council or any standing committee appointed by the Council shall be three years from the date of appointment or nomination as the case may be, provided that a member appointed or nominated in his/her capacity as a member of a particular body or as the holder of a particular appointment shall automatically cease to be member if he/she ceases to be a member of that body or the holder of that appointment. Any person appointed to a casual vacancy among the non-official members of the Council for the residue of the term for which the person whose place he/she fills would have been a member.

1.8 PROCEEDINGS OF THE COUNCIL

(i) The Chairperson of the Council, when present, shall preside over all meetings of the Council.

(ii) In the absence of the Chairperson, the Secretary, Ministry of Labour, shall preside. On occasions when the Chairperson/Secretary, Ministry of Labour, is unable to preside over a meeting of the Council, the members present shall elect a Chairperson from amongst themselves for that particular meeting.

(iii) One-third of the number of members of the Council shall constitute the quorum for any meeting of the Council.

(iv) Not less than 30 days' notice of every meeting of the Council shall ordinarily be given to each member, but a shorter notice may be given for urgent meetings. The Council shall meet as often as may be necessary and at least once in every year.

(v) The agenda of every meeting shall be sent so as to reach the members at least 15 days before the scheduled date of the meeting.

(vi) In the case of difference of opinion among the members of the Council, the opinion of the majority shall prevail.

(vii) If there is equality of votes, the President of the meeting shall exercise a casting vote.

(viii) The Chairperson, may, in special circumstances, instead of convening a meeting of the Council, obtain the views of the members on any item of business individually by circulation instead of at a meeting.

(ix) No proceedings of the Council shall be invalidated merely by reason of the existence of any vacancy or vacancies among the members.

1.9 COMMITTEES

The Council shall have the power to appoint committees for assisting it in the discharge of its functions. The recommendation of sub-committees must be ratified by the main council.

The recommendations of the Council on training policies shall be referred to the Government of India for decisions.

1.10 TRADE TESTS

Trade tests in various courses will be arranged by or under the authority of the National Council for Vocational Training and certificates duly approved by it will be awarded to successful candidates.

1.11 INSPECTION OF TRAINING INSTITUTES

The Council's functions with regard to inspection of training institutes shall be exercised through the State Directorate of Training. Training institutions which have already been affiliated or which have applied for affiliation by the National Council shall afford all facilities for inspection to the staff of the Directorate of Training or any member of the National Council examining body in a state or of any committee appointed by the National Council.

1.12 NCVT SECRETARIAT

The Directorate of Training, Ministry of Labour, Government of India, shall provide the required secretarial assistance to the Council.

1.13 PUBLICATIONS

An annual report of the working of the National Council for Vocational Training shall be published. The Council may also publish periodicals and news bulletins for disseminating information of interest to trainees and training institutions and industries.

1.14 FINANCIAL ASPECTS

The expenses of the Council shall be met by the Government of India. Official members of the Council and of the committees will draw travelling and other allowances for attending the Council's meetings and for performing work connected with the Council from their respective governments. Non-official members of the Council will be paid travelling allowances by the Government of India at the rate admissible to Government of India officers of the first grade in accordance with the supplementary rules.

1.15 SUB-COMMITTEES OF NCVT

1. Evaluation of Training Programmes of Government and Private ITIs

As recommended by the NCVT in its seventh meeting held in November 1965, the issue of formation of sub-committees of the National Council for evaluation of ITIs with a view to making definite suggestions for the improvement of standards of training, has been considered by the Government of India. It has been decided to set up one such sub-committees in each state/union territory.

The composition of the sub-committee is given below (five members):

(i) Director General of Employment and Training or his/her nominee
(ii) State Director In-charge of CTS
(iii) One member nominated by All India Council for Technical Education
(iv) One member nominated by an employers' organization
(v) One member nominated by a workers' organization

2. Sub-Committees of NCVT for Affiliation of ITIs

The standing committee reports for grant of affiliation to trades/units of the ITIs is considered by a sub-committee of NCVT dealing with affiliation of ITIs. The composition of the sub-committee of NCVT dealing with affiliation is as follows:

1.	DG/JS,DGE&T		Chairperson
2.	DDG(T)		Vice-Chairperson
3.	Central Departments/Ministries	2 members	Nominated by rotation for a period of one year
4.	Representatives from State Governments/UT Administrations	4 members, one each from four regions	Nominated by rotation for a period of one year
5.	Representative from NE states	1 member	Nominated by rotation from NE states and Sikkim for a period of one year
6.	Representative from employers' organisations	1 member	Nominated by rotation for a period of one year
7.	Representative from workers' organisations	1 member	Nominated by rotation for a period of one year
8.	Representative from professional and learned bodies	1 member	Nominated by rotation for a period of one year
9.	Experts	1 member	Nominated by rotation for a period of one year
10	Representative from SC/ST	1 member	Nominated by rotation for a period of one year
11	Women	1 member	
11	Director Training		Member Secretary
		Total—16 members	

The sub-committee of the NCVT will be reconstituted after the expiry of three years from the date of its constitution and only members of the working NCVT will be nominated on this sub-committee.

3. Sub-Committee for Norms and Courses

A sub-committee of the NCVT for norms and courses has been set up with the following functions:

(i) Study of existing trades covered and evaluation of their curricula to enhance their relevance to industry
(ii) Suggest introduction of new trades and discontinue obsolete ones
(iii) Modification/revision in course material of existing trades
(iv) Revamping the curriculum of any trade above the NCVT's norms on the basis of industry needs
(v) Regular interaction with industry /industry associations to assess the training needs
(vi) Establishment of proven mechanism for periodic revision of curricula
(vii) Qualitative improvement in present skill training by adding basic/life skills/communication skills in existing course curricula
(viii) To discusses issues relating to norms or standards or policy matter before circulation to all members for approval

The following should be the composition of sub-committee of NCVT for norms and courses:

1. DG/JS, DGE&T	Chairperson
2. DDG (T)	Vice-Chairperson
3. Director Training	Member
4. Representative of DIT in NCVT	Member
5. Representative of MOIA in NCVT	Member
6. Representative from HRD in NCVT	Member
7. State Director of TN	Member
8. State Director of Gujarat	Member
9. State Director of West Bengal	Member
10. Representatives of CII/FICCI/ASSOCHAM	Member
11. Representative of BMS	Member
12. Expert (on rotation basis)	Member
13. Experts from Industries (according to requirement) (maximum up to 4)	Co-opt members
14. Director, NIMI	Member
15. Representative from AICTE	Member
16. Director, CSTARI	Member
17. Director Training	Member Secretary

1.16 STATE COUNCIL FOR VOCATIONAL TRAINING AS SOCIETY

The State Council corresponding to the National Council deals with all matters relating to vocational training at State level.

Objective The State Council, which is affiliated to the National Council for Vocational Training, functions as a state agency to advise the state government, in carrying out the training policy laid down by the National Council and to co-ordinate the vocational training programme throughout the state.

Functions

(i) To carry out the policy of the National Council with regard to the award of National Trade Certificates in engineering and non-engineering trades as may be brought within its scope by the central or state government

(ii) To implement the decision and carry out the policy laid down by the National Council in respect of syllabi, equipment, scale of accommodation, duration of courses and method of training

(iii) To establish State Board of Examination in vocational trades

(iv) To arrange for ad-hoc or periodical inspection of the training institutes in the state and ensure that the standards prescribed by the National Council are being followed

(v) To co-opt, if necessary, any person or persons to advise the State Council in connection with its work

(vi) To ensure that the staff is employed according to the qualifications prescribed by the National Council and relax qualifications in special circumstances to be recorded, for trades where such staff is not easily available

(vii) To ensure that the examinations are conducted by the State Board of Examinations according to standards and the manner prescribed by the National Council

(viii) To counter-sign and issue the National Trade Certificates to successful candidates
(ix) To recommend the provision of additional training facilities, wherever necessary, and render such assistance in the setting up of additional training programmes as may be necessary
(x) To advise the state government regarding expenditure on different training schemes
(xi) To perform such other functions as may be entrusted to it by the state government

1.17 REGISTRATION OF SCVT AS SOCIETY

The State Governments to ensure that SCVT is registered as a Society in their respective state, with separate website and bank account, which should be audited regularly. A draft Memorandum of Article and Association for society is given at (**Appendix-I**).

DGE&T-19(13)/2011-CD dated 28th March, 2011

1.18 BOARD OF EXAMINATIONS

The State Council shall constitute a Board of Examination as a committee of the State Council, which shall perform the following functions:

(i) To constitute a Local Board of Examination at each examination centre
(ii) To co-opt outside experts on the Local Board of Examination as and when necessary
(iii) To make necessary arrangements for the proper conduct of examinations including the provision of raw materials, answer books and other stationery at the examination centre
(iv) To fix the scale of remuneration of the outside experts on the Local Board of Examination and arrange payment thereof
(v) To ensure compliance with the standards prescribed by the National Council for the conduct of the examination
(vi) To declare final results
(vii) To submit a yearly report to the State Council regarding its activities and to suggest measures for effecting improvements

1.19 ROLE OF THE DIRECTORATE GENERAL OF EMPLOYMENT AND TRAINING (DGE&T)

Vocational and technical training of labour is a part of the concurrent list of the Constitution of India (Entry 25). As per allocation of Business Rule, 1961, the Ministry of Labour and Employment is charged with the responsibility of vocational training of labour. The responsibility is discharged through the Directorate General of Employment and Training, which is a subsidiary office within the Ministry of Labour and Employment.

The Directorate General of Resettlement and Employment (DGR&E), now known as the Directorate General of Employment and Training (DGE&T), was set up in 1945 for resettling demobilised defense service personnel and discharged war workers in civilian life. After independence in 1947, the Directorate General was also called upon to handle work relating to displaced persons from Pakistan. Subsequently, the scope of the Directorate General was extended to cover employment service to all categories of jobseekers in early 1948, and training services to all civilians in 1950.

The Directorate General of Employment and Training (DGE&T) in the Ministry of Labour and Employment is an apex organisation for development and coordination of vocational training. It includes vocational training for women and employable persons in the country and providing skilled manpower to the industry besides providing employment services. DGE&T offers a range of training courses catering to the needs of different segments of society. Courses are available for school-leavers, ITI passed-outs, ITI instructors, industrial workers, technicians, junior and middle-level executives, supervisors/foremen, women, physically disabled persons and Scheduled Castes and Scheduled Tribes (SCs/STs). It also conducts training-oriented research and development of instructional media packages for the use of trainees and instructors. The Craftsmen Training Scheme (CTS) is one of the schemes implemented by DGE&T for school-leavers.

Chapter 2

Craftsmen Training Scheme (CTS)

2.1 INTRODUCTION

The Government of India introduced the Craftsmen Training Scheme (CTS) in 1950 to ensure a steady flow of skilled workers in different trades for the domestic industry. The objectives was to raise quantitatively and qualitatively the industrial production by systematic training, to reduce unemployment among the educated youth by providing them employable training, and to cultivate and nurture a technical and industrial attitude in the minds of the younger generation. The Scheme, the most important in the field of vocational training, has been shaping craftsmen to meet the existing as well as future manpower need, through the vast network of ITIs in the various states/union territories of the country.

The day-to-day administration of ITIs under the Craftsmen Training Scheme was transferred to the state governments/union territory administrations with effect from the year 1956. The financial control of industrial training institutes in the states as well as in the union territories has been transferred to the respective state government/union territory on 1 April, 1969. Financial assistance is granted to them in the form of a bulk grant in consultation with the Planning Commission and the Ministry of Finance.

2.2 GROWTH OF ITIs IN THE COUNTRY

The Craftsmen Training Scheme (CTS) was initiated by the Directorate General of Employment and Training (DGE&T), Ministry of Labour and Employment, in 1950 by establishing about 50 Industrial Training Institutes (ITIs) for imparting skills in various vocational trades to meet the skilled manpower requirement for industrial growth of the country. Several private ITIs were established in the 1980's in southern states, mostly in Kerala, Karnataka and Andhra Pradesh, from where trained craftsmen found placement in the Gulf countries. In the year 1980, there were 831 ITIs which have grown to 10,750 with seating capacity of 15.24 lakhs as on 31 December, 2013.

2.3 OBJECTIVES OF THE SCHEME

The objectives of the Craftsmen Training Scheme are

(i) To equip the human resource with appropriate skills required in the labour market

(ii) To make the youth more productive by providing them employable skills to achieve wage benefits as well as self-employment

(iii) To produce highly skilled craftsmen for the industry

(iv) To ensure steady flow of skilled workers for industrial/service sectors

(v) To raise the quality and quantity of industrial production by systematic training of potential workers

2.4 SALIENT FEATURES OF THE SCHEME

The Craftsmen Training Scheme (CTS) is a major scheme catering to the need of school-leavers and forms the backbone of the National Vocational Training System of the country. State government departments deliver vocational training to school-leavers through ITIs.

(i) Government Industrial Training Institutes are under the administrative and financial control of the respective State Governments.

(ii) Private Industrial Training Institutes are privately funded and managed. However, some of them get support from respective State Governments.

(iii) Candidates of 14 years of age or higher are eligible to seek admission in ITIs. There is no upper age limit for admission to ITIs affiliated to NCVT. Semester System in place of existing long term courses have been introduced w.e.f. session strartel from August 2013.

(iv) Admissions in ITIs are done twice a year, i.e. in the months of August and February.

(v) About 70% of the training period is allotted to practical training and the rest to subjects relating to Trade Theory, Workshop Calculation and Science/Engineering Drawing, and Employability Skills.

(vi) Tuition fee in ITIs is decided by the respective State Government as deemed fit, based on the recommendation of the concerned State Council for Vocational Training. Tuition fee in case of institutes under DGE&T/UT Administration is ₹100/- per month per trainee. However, no fee is being charged currently from SC/ST candidates and persons of disadvantaged groups.

(vii) There is a provision for grant of stipend to the trainees of government ITIs. They are also provided with a library, sports and medical facilities. Some State Governments levy a nominal fee for the purpose.

(viii) Seats are reserved for SC/ST candidates in proportion to their population in the respective state/UT. Guidelines for reserving 3% seats for persons with disabilities and 30% for female candidates have been issued to State Governments and these could be filled based on the general reservation policy of each state/UT, and the total reservation is limited to 50%. Seats are also reserved for the wards of defence personnel. Seats for OBC candidates have also been reserved in proportion to the seats reserved for them in government services in the respective states.

(ix) For optimum utilization of available infrastructural facilities, there is a provision of second and third shifts in ITIs with segregated timing. The institutes are encouraged to introduce second shifts by appointing one additional trade instructor and additional trainee kits for trainees.

(x) A placement cell in every ITI is set up to facilitate the graduates in getting placements in different industries.

2.5 MULTI-SKILL COURSES UNDER CRAFTSMEN TRAINING SCHEME

As a paradigm shift in Craftsmen Training System in the country, a multi-skilling multi-entry and exit vocational training program can be offered in ITIs. As per norms, Broad Based Basic Training (multi-skill) courses are offered during the first year followed by Advanced and Specialized Modular Courses of 6 months' duration each in the second year of training. The training programme is designed to cater to training needs of particular group of industries. The structure of the training course is as under:

(i) "Broad Based Basic Training" (BBBT) in a number of skill areas related to a particular industrial sector during first year.
(ii) Advanced modular courses of 6 months' duration in the second year.
(iii) The curriculum for the above-mentioned BBBT as well as Advanced Modular Courses of 6 months' duration is available at http://dget.nic.in/coe/main/index.htm. Trade testing for these courses is done at the national level under the aegis of National Council for Vocational Training (NCVT). Examination Guidelines and Marking Scheme is given in **Chapter 4**.
(iv) National Trade Certificates of one-year Broad Based Basic Training as well as for Advanced Modules are awarded to the successful trainees.
(v) Specialized modular courses are organised during the last phase of training to bridge the skill gaps keeping in view the needs of industry in the region. The testing and certification for the last phase is done jointly by State Governments and Industry. These certificates are recognized by the NCVT. Detailed Guidelines and certificate are given at **(Appendix XII)**.
(vi) List of sectors and modules covered so far is given at **(Appendix XIII)**.
(vii) Trainees of COE can also opt courses under Apprenticeship Trying Scheme after completely 1 year BBBT and 6 month advanced modem. List of trader cover under ATS is at **(Appendix XIV)**.

2.6 RESPONSIBILITIES OF CENTRAL AND STATE GOVERNMENTS FOR IMPLEMENTATION OF CTS

1. Responsibilities of the Central Government

(i) Framing of overall policies, norms and standards for training
(ii) Formulation of new training schemes for qualitative and quantitative upgradation of the Craftsmen Training Scheme
(iii) Development of course curricula
(iv) Affiliation of training institutes, i.e. ITIs
(v) Trade testing and certification
(vi) Conducting craft instructor training courses for serving and potential instructors of ITIs
(vii) Conducting courses for skill upgradation of industrial workers by offering short-term and long-term courses in specialized fields
(viii) Implementation and regulation of training for trade apprentices under the Apprentices Act, 1961
(ix) Organizing vocational training programmes for women
(x) Implementing international agreements and facilitating cooperation in the field of vocational training

2. Responsibilities of State Governments

(i) Day-to-day administration of Industrial Training Institutes
(ii) Implementation of Craftsmen Training Schemes in ITIs
(iii) Conducting training courses in ITIs
(iv) Setting up of new institutes, addition of trade units in the existing institutes as per requirement of local industries
(v) Arrangements for smooth conduction of trade tests, evaluation and award of certificates
(vi) Implementation of central schemes in their respective states

2.7 ADMINISTRATION AND CONDUCT OF TRAINING PROGRAMMES IN INDUSTRIAL TRAINING INSTITUTES

Transfer of Control of ITIs to States

The financial control of Industrial Training Institutes in states as well as union territories has been transferred to the respective State Governments/Union Territories on 1 April, 1969. Financial assistance is granted to them under various schemes formulated in consultation with the Planning Commission, the Ministry of Finance and other concerned ministries/departments.

Survey of Occupations Around ITIs for Determining the Scope for Training in the ITIs

The points which may have to be taken into consideration while deciding to set up an ITI, introducing trades or suggesting the closure of the unpopular trades and substituting them with more popular trades, a survey of occupations around ITIs for determining the Scope for Training in the ITIs (Industry-wise Survey) may be undertaken as per (**Appendix V**).

2.8 TRAINING IN GOVT. /PVT. ITIs

Skill-training programmes under government and private ITIs have been designed to impart basic skills and knowledge in trades so as to prepare trainees as semi-skilled workers for wage employment as well as self-employment.

About 70% of the training period is allotted to practical training and the rest to subjects relating to Trade Theory, Workshop Calculation and Science, and Engineering Drawing. An emphasis is on skill building; therefore, most of the time is devoted to practical training. In order to impart awareness on issues like workers' rights, occupational safety and health, soft skills, entrepreneurship and IT literacy, a compulsory subject. "Employability Skills" in place of "Social Studies" has been introduced w.e.f. August 2012 in all government and private ITIs.

(DGE&T-19/17/2010-CD, dated 15.04.2011)

Semester System

All the Government and Private ITIs have been advised to implement training programme under semester system in place of existing long term courses. The detail guide line for implementation of semester system are:

- Craftsmen Training System in semester pattern will be imparted as per the syllabi approved by the NCVT for each semester.
- The complete course of Craftsmen Training for all the trades (Engineering & Non-Engineering) will be delivered in one to four semesters each of six months duration depending upon the trade.
- Training in any semester is to be started from an academic session i.e. either in the month of August or February.
- On completion of the training period of a particular semester, Trade Testing would be done under the aegis of NCVT in July and January every year.
- Examination for each semester both for theory, Workshop Calculation & Science, Engineering Drawing, Employability Skills and trade practical will be conducted based on the syllabus of the corresponding semester.

- A consolidated mark-sheet would be issued by respective State Government after completing all the semesters based on marks obtained in each semester examination.
- For award of NTC, a trainee has to secure pass marks in each subject in each semester.

DGE&T 19(4)/2011–CD(Dt) [17/January/14th March, 2013]

2.9 ADMISSION IN GOVERNMENT AND PRIVATE ITIs

1. Age

Candidates who have attained the age of 14 years as on the date of commencement of an academic session are eligible for admission in ITIs affiliated to NCVT.

There is no upper age limit for trainees seeking admission in courses under Craftsmen Training Scheme.

(DGE&T-19(15) / 2010-CD, dated 20.9.2010)

2. Qualification

Persons having educational qualifications as VIII/X/XII pass can take admission in ITIs. The required minimum qualifications are prescribed in the respective trade syllabi, as well as in the list of Trades under Craftsmen Training Scheme (CTS) given at **(Appendix VII)**.

3. Reservation of Seats

This should be as follows:

(i) Seats for candidates belonging to Scheduled Castes/Tribes are in proportion to their population in each State/Union Territory.

(ii) Seats are reserved for OBC candidates in ITIs keeping in view the overall reservation policy of the respective states.

(DGE&T-19(12)/2002-CD, dated 15.11.2002)

(iii) 30% seats are horizontally reserved for female candidates in each category and these seats can be filled up based on the general reservation policy of each state/UT. If the seats meant for them are not utilized fully, the same can be filled in by male candidates subsequently.

(DGE&T-19(27)/2007-CD, dated 2.6.2008)

(iv) For boys and girls sponsored by recognized orphanages, if specific reservation is not possible, at least preference should be given to them at the time of admission to Industrial Training Institutes.

(v) 3% of the seats for admission into the Craftsmen Training Scheme should be reserved for candidates who are differently abled but have aptitude and are otherwise fit to undergo the required training. Attempts may be made by the states/UTs to ensure that 3% of the seats reserved for the differently abled are fully utilized. Steps should also be taken to give wide publicity in this regard, also by bringing this fact to the notice of associations/organizations of differently abled persons and located in the states. However, these students should be admitted only in those trades categorized in the list of trades with PWD categories as given at **(Appendix IX)** as per the type of disability.

(DGE&T-19(19)/90-CD, dated 10.5.90)

For Wards of Defence Personnel

(vi) The Directorate General of Resettlement has confirmed the inclusion of ex-servicemen category in the revised priorities for reservation up to 10 seats in each ITI. As such, the revised priorities for admission of wards of defence personnel, etc., would henceforth be as under:

(a) Children of deceased/disabled ex-servicemen, including those killed/disabled during peace time
(b) Children of ex-servicemen
(c) Children of serving jawans
(d) Children of serving officers
(e) Ex-servicemen

(DGE&T-29/ (4)/86-CD, dated April, 1986)

(vii) 10 seats are kept reserved in each of the 410 identified ITIs with a maximum of 2 seats in a trade for Defence Service Personnel under pre-cum-post release training programme in ITIs from the session starting August 2000. The list would be submitted by DGR for each state to the concerned State Directorate well in advance to enable them to reserve the seats in different ITIs. For ITIs meant for women, only women candidates, if any, would be considered for admission. The State Directorate would issue necessary instructions to the principals of the concerned ITIs to reserve seats in the trades as per the request of DGR. Where it is not possible to accommodate the request, admission in alternative ITIs could be given.

(DGE&T-7/1/2000-TC, dated 22.6.2000)

4. Admission

Admission will be made purely on merit, based on the marks secured by candidates in the public examination of the minimum qualification prescribed for the respective trade. Wherever there is no public examination at the minimum qualification level, the selection will be made on merit, based on the marks obtained by the candidates in the written examination conducted by the State Directorate for this purpose.

(DGE&T-19(28)/96-CD, dated 4.6.97)

Selection of candidates for admission in Industrial Training Institutes should start well in advance of the commencement of each session. Admission should be completed as per the following schedule. Trade-wise details of trainees admitted in the institute should be submitted to DGE&T immediately after closing the admission by sending a soft copy in CD/e-mail to Director of Training.

(i) Cut-off date for admission in August session—31 August of the year
(ii) Cut-off date for admission in February session—28 February of the year

5. Supernumeraries

The percentage of supernumeraries to be admitted should be decided with the object of fully utilizing the sanctioned seats at each institute. There is provision of 30% supernumerary seats in government and private ITIs for both engineering and non-engineering trades. To take care of drop-out and to ensure optimum utilization of the available infrastructure created for training, without compromising on the quality of training, institutes are allowed to admit 30% more trainees at the time of admission only and not in between the session.

(DGE&T 19(20)/2007-CD, dated 2.6.2008)

(i) Fees for Application Form and Registration

(a) Application form—₹25/- (₹ twenty-five only)
(b) Registration fee—₹50/- (₹ fifty only)

(DGE&T-19(10)/2002-CD, dated 19/24.12.2002)

(ii) Tuition Fees

(a) ₹100/- per month per trainee has been prescribed as tuition fee. Tuition fee in the case of ITIs is to be decided by the respective State Government as deemed fit based on the recommendation of the concerned State Council for Vocational Training.
(b) Tuition fee in the case of institutes under DGE&T/Union Territory administration is ₹100/- per month or part thereof per trainee.

(DGE&T-19/(10)/2002-CD, dated 19.12.2002)

(c) No fee is charged from SC/ST and physically handicapped trainees.

(DGE&T-19(13)/95-CD, dated 30.7.96)

(d) The State Directors/UTs in consultation with SCVT will decide suitable tuition fee to be charged by private ITIs keeping in the view the cost of training.

(DGE&T-19(18)/95-CD, dated 6.8.96)

(iii) Caution Money

(a) To guard against the loss or damage to equipment, tools and other articles entrusted to a trainee's charge, each candidate is required to deposit to the head of the training institute, a sum of ₹250/- as caution money at the time of joining the institute is at **(Appendix-XIVA)**.

(DGE&T-19(10)/2002-CD, dated 19.12.2002)

Ordinarily, the caution money should be deposited in full by the trainees at the time of their admission. In deserving cases, however, the State Director may make a relaxation to the extent that the amount is realized in suitable installments within one month of a candidate's admission. The caution money should be kept intact. Any recoveries from the trainees that may be necessary on account of damage to or loss of tools and equipment should be made in cash or by other means. Utilization of caution money should be resorted to only in those cases where a trainee has left or is leaving an institute and is otherwise unable to pay.

The caution money deposited by the trainees of the ITIs may be refunded to them as soon as they complete the institutional training and hand over the tools and other articles entrusted to them. A certificate from the instructor concerned to the effect that no article belonging to the institute is left with the trainees, should, however, be produced by them along with the application for the refund of the caution money.

(DGE&T-29(1)/86-CD, dated 17.2.86)

(b) To guard against the loss or damage to hostel articles, each hostel boarder of an ITI will also be required to deposit with the head of the training institute a sum of ₹125/- only as 'Hostel Caution Money' and ₹10/- only per year as 'Hostel Service Charges'.

(DGE&T-19(10)/2002-CD, dated 19.12.2002)

Both the caution amounts deposited by the trainees may be refunded to them in the event of their discharge from the institute/hostel on any ground.

(c) All deposits should be refunded normally on satisfactory completion of the institutional training.

(d) All balances unclaimed for more than three complete account years from the date they first become repayable, shall at the close of March in each year, be credited to the government as unclaimed deposits.

(e) The date of the first repayment shall be the date on which a trainee successfully completes the training.

(f) Caution money will be forfeited in the case of trainees who discontinue their training after one month of commencement of training.

(DGE&T-12(8)/75-TC, dated 6.2.76)

(iv) Medical Examination

(a) Trainees should be medically examined soon after their admission by the Medical Officer attached to the ITI. They should also be examined, thereafter once in a year. In case of trainees with doubtful health, the medical examination may be held every three months. At training institutes, where no medical officer has been appointed, arrangements for medical examination may be made through a local doctor. For this purpose, the State Director may sanction an examination fee at a rate not exceeding ₹25/- per trainee examined on each occasion, besides conveyance charges. Training institutes within two and a half kilometres of one another may be treated as one centre in calculating the rate of fee to be paid. The head of the training institute should discharge trainees found medically unfit on admission. The case of differently abled persons with specified limitations shall be examined by the State Government/Union Territory administrators concerned on merits, for relaxation of standards referred to above.

(DGE&T-19(10)/2002-CD, dated 19.12.2002)

(b) No rigid physical standards have been prescribed for admission under the Craftsmen Training Scheme. A trainee with contagious and infectious diseases should not be admitted. Proper publicity should be given to inform prospective trainees about physical standards/norms required for employment, so that candidates are fully aware of the requirements before seeking admission.

(DGE&T-19(11)/91-CD, dated 6.1.92)

(v) Aptitude Test

(a) An aptitude test may be conducted for candidates selected for admission into Industrial Training Institutes at the end of the second month after admission. If a candidate is found unsuitable for a particular trade, he/she should be considered for admission in any other trade before rejecting him/her altogether.

(b) Trainees may be allowed a change of trade within the first month of their admission to a training institute provided they possess the requisite qualifications for the new trade and vacancies are available.

(c) The use of aptitude test is optional and left to the State Government.

(DGE&T-19(10)/92-CD, dated 7.7.92)

(vi) Transfer of Trainees The State Director may sanction the transfer of a trainee willing to get transferred from one training institute to another or the exchange of trainees between training institutes provided the sanctioned distribution of trades and the sanctioned number of trainees at those institutes are unaffected and such transfers do not involve any expenditure on travelling, etc.

(vii) Facilities to Trainees Trainees will be given the following facilities wherever available in the institute on deposit of nominal gymkhana fee to be decided by the principal of the institute.

(a) Games and recreation facilities and medical treatment

(b) Subsidized hostel accommodation

(c) Medical treatment

2.10 GENERAL GUIDELINES FOR TRAINING IN ITIs

1. Working Hours

It has been decided that the number of working hours at the ITIs should be fixed at 7½ hours per day with the second Saturday of a month as a holiday.

(i) Total working hours: 42 hours per week.

(ii) Practical Instruction: 28 hours per week.

(iii) Theoretical Instruction: 10 hours per week as per following break up:

(a) Trade Theory	4 hours per week
(b) Workshop Calculation and Science	2 hours per week
(c) Engineering Drawing	2 hours per week
(d) Employability Skills	2 hours per week
(e) Extracurricular activities including Library Studies and Physical Training/Sports	4 hours per week

(DGE&T-12(19)/83-TC, dated 12.10.83)

2. Minimum Compulsory Attendance for Trainees

(i) The minimum compulsory attendance for trainees regarding their eligibility for the final trade test has been fixed at 80% of the actual number of working days.

(ii) For purpose of calculating 80% of the actual number of working days in respect of a trainee, actual number of working days will be the number of days for which attendance was marked in the attendance register during the period between the day of his/her admission and the date of the beginning of the trade test. There may be cases in which the attendance of a trainee falls short of 80% due to reasons beyond his/her control. In such cases, no fixed rules can be laid down. If a trainee has not missed essential training, the shortage of attendance, if due to causes beyond his/her control, may be condoned.

(iii) Where a trainee absents himself/herself for more than half the number of days, for whatever reasons, he/she should not be allowed to continue his training. Where, however, the absence is due to unavoidable circumstances and the trainee has the required aptitude and capacity to become a skilled craftsperson, the State Director in-charge of the training scheme should decide each case on its own merits and admit the candidate for further training along with the senior batch provided there are vacancies in the concerned trade. The re-admitted trainee will not be allowed a stipend.

(iv) The hours lost on the shop floor by a trainee due to absence over and above the prescribed minimum of 80% attendance should be made up by the trainees by working in the shift to the extent necessary to make up the loss in training without providing any additional equipment and staff. The assignments to the trainee may be made by his/her instructors and the work may be supervised by the instructors in charge of the shift in which the trainee works. This concession should, however, be given only to those trainees who lose training for reasons beyond their control and not for those who remain absent frequently for trivial reasons.

3. Holidays

(i) Trainees may be allowed the same holidays as fixed by the State Director for observance by the staff. If a trainee is a stipend holder, he/she would be paid stipend at the full rate during such holidays.

(ii) With a view to have uniformity in the working of ITIs all over the country, there will be no winter/summer holidays as such but the State Government may close institutes that are in inaccessible/snow-bound areas for a period not exceeding 15 days in a year. Efforts should be made to complete the loss due to such closure by working extra hours during the year. This closure need not therefore apply to all the ITIs even if they are in the same state.

(DGE&T-12(15)/77-TC, dated 28.5.77)

4. Leave Admissible to Trainees

(i) Casual Leave

(a) Casual leave at the rate of 12 days per year for courses of one-year training duration or more will be admissible subject to a maximum of 10 days at any one time.

(b) For courses of 6-month duration, only 6 days of casual leave are admissible.

(c) Any holiday falling during the period of casual leave shall not be counted for the purpose of the limit of 12 days.

(d) Casual leave not utilized during the first year of a 2-year course shall stand lapsed at the end of the first year and shall not be permitted to be carried forward to the second year. If the trainee is a stipend holder, he/she will continue to draw the stipend at full rate during the period of casual leave. Casual leave cannot be combined with any other kind of leave. If casual leave is preceded or followed by medical or special leave, the entire leave taken will be treated as medical or special leave provided that it shall not be allowed to exceed the maximum leave prescribed in respect of medical/special leave.

(ii) Medical Leave

(a) 15 days of medical leave is allowed to trainees unable to attend duty owing to illness other than injuries received while at work.

(b) Leave for a further period not exceeding three weeks for one-year trade courses and six weeks for two-year trade courses in addition to 15 days of absence may be granted to a trainee on producing a medical certificate from a medical officer or a registered medical practitioner. This leave should only be granted once during the period of training.

(c) A trainee who requires extension of leave beyond 15 days and who does not go to a hospital for treatment, may be granted leave on the recommendations of the medical officer, if any, posted at the training institute by the State Government or a medical officer not below the rank of Assistant Surgeon.

(d) If the medical officer of the rank of Assistant Surgeon is not within easy reach of the trainee, a certificate signed by a registered medical practitioner may be accepted. The cost of medical treatment, seat rent, etc., will be borne by the Government in the case of a trainee admitted as an indoor patient in a hospital. The cost of diet during his/her stay as an indoor patient in a hospital will be borne by the trainee and not by the Government. The principal of the training institute will arrange to pay the hospital bill after obtaining the sanction of the concerned State Director, if necessary. A trainee who holds a stipend will be allowed to draw stipend at the full rate during such leave.

(e) During illness, trainees residing in government hostels will also be paid actual conveyance charge to and from the hospital by the cheapest mode of conveyance, irrespective of whether they are admitted in the hospital as indoor patients or not.

(f) Trainees who are not fit for duty or do not report for duty at the end of two months should be discharged from the date of expiry of the period. They may, however, be readmitted for training by the State Director at his/her discretion, provided he/she is satisfied that they could not join earlier and that they will be able to complete their course within the prescribed period. Any period involved in excess of the leave admissible will be without stipend in the case of trainees who hold a stipend.

(g) In no circumstances should patent medicines be allowed to trainees at the cost of the Government. The term 'patent medicine' means medicines not ordinarily stocked in local government hospitals or dispensaries but does not include vaccine, sera, or other materials required for injections, provided they are administered on a limited scale as part of treatment for specific ailments and the necessity for their use is certified by a competent medical officer.

(DGE&T-19(12)/90-CD, dated 25.5.90)

(iii) Special Leave Special leave of up to 10 days for private reasons may be allowed to a trainee. In extraordinary cases, where the head of the institute is satisfied that the requirement is genuine, the period of special leave may, at his/her discretion, be raised to a maximum of 15 days for trainees of one-year trade courses and 30 days for trainees of two-year trade courses. No scholarship will be admissible during the period of special leave to a trainee who is a scholarship holder.

(DGE&T-19(12)/90-CD, dated 25.5.90)

If a trainee overstays the maximum period of special leave, he/she should be struck off the rolls from the day following the date of expiry of the period and treated as an absconder.

(iv) Training Fee of Leave Period Training fee will be payable to industrial training institutes with regard to trainees who avail of the above kinds of leave.

(v) Unauthorized Absence For unauthorized absence of less than 10 consecutive days at a time, the principal of the institute should issue a written warning to the trainee for the first occasion. If the offence is repeated, his/her case should be reported to the State Director, with a view to discharge. Proportionate deduction of stipend from such trainees who are stipend holders should be made by the principal of the institute for all unauthorized absence.

(vi) Absconders A trainee who absents himself from a training institute for 10 consecutive days without permission and without informing the principal of the institute of the reasons for his/her absence, should be treated as an absconder and struck off the rolls with effect from the first day of his/her absence. If a trainee returns to the training institute within two weeks after having been struck off as an absconder, he/she may be re-admitted by the principal of the institute with the approval of the State Director, provided the trainee gives a satisfactory explanation of his/her absence.

(vii) Suspensions, Discharges and Resignations

(a) State Directors may discharge, at their discretion. such trainees as are recommended for discharge by principals of training institutes on account of unsatisfactory progress in training, misconduct, etc. For acts of indiscipline and misconduct, the principal of the institute should issue a written warning for the first offence. If the offence is repeated, the trainee's case should be reported to the State Director with a view to discharge.

(b) Pending investigation of allegations against a trainee suspected of misconduct, he/she may be suspended by the principal of the training institute for good and proper reasons which should be recorded by the principal in writing. During the period of suspension, no stipend should be paid to a trainee suspended for misconduct. The stipend may, however, be paid in full if and when such a trainee is exonerated.

(c) Where a trainee under suspension is subsequently exonerated and the attendance due to his/her suspension falls short of the prescribed 80% limit, he/she may be allowed to complete his/her training, notwithstanding the shortage, and allowed to sit for the trade test if he/she has covered the prescribed training course.

5. Award of Stipend

(a) A stipend of ₹100/- per month per trainee may be awarded to all trainees with approval of the Finance Department of the respective State Government. However, the State Government is at their liberty to increase the rate of stipend.

(DGE&T-19 (12)/95-CD, dated 2.9.96)

(b) In addition to the normal stipend mentioned above, merit scholarships at the rate of ₹125/- per month per trainee may also be awarded to 4% of the total number of trainees on the rolls (both engineering and non-engineering trades) on the basis of internal examination to be conducted at each Industrial Training Institute.

(DGE&T-19(8)/99-CD), dated 7.1. 2000)

(c) Stipends should be granted to trainees only after the aptitude tests are over and decisions taken regarding the discharge of supernumeraries. The award of stipends should be finalized within a period of about three months of the start of the session.

6. Supply of Stationary to Trainees Trainees in the trades of Draughtsman (Civil and Mechanical) and Surveyor will be supplied with the following articles:

(a) One pencil—medium hard	Every month
(b) One blank drawing book (24 pages)	Every two months
(c) One eraser	Every three months
(d) Laboratory-size exercise book (one side blank and the other side ruled)	One per session
(e) Drawing sheets	As required

The cost of the stationary will be met as follows:

(a) Government Industrial Training Institutes from training grant
(b) Private Industrial Training Institutes from training fees

(DGE&T-19(14)/93-CD, dated 23.9.93)

7. Supply of Overalls (Workshop Clothing) After every six months, one overall may be provided to trainees required to work on or near machines. So far as trainees of Draftsman (Mechanical and Civil) and Surveyor trades are concerned, they may be provided with one overall during the course of training. Workshop attendants can also be provided with one overall every year. It is left to the respective State Governments to decide for themselves the quality of cloth, according to the availability of cloth in their local markets. No monetary limits are fixed for this purpose.

(DGE&T-19(8)/92-CD, dated 25.6.92)

8. Sale of Manufactured Products As per respective State Government rules.

9. Manufacture of Certain Items of Tools and Equipment at Industrial Training Institutes by Trainees

(a) Trainees at ITIs are required to carry out graded exercises to learn the skills of their trades progressively. It is felt that during the practical work done by the trainees, certain items included in the list of tools and equipment as well as some furniture can be easily manufactured with the raw material out of the training grant provided for the purpose of training. Items which can be conveniently manufactured during the training may be chosen from the list of tools and equipment with respect to various trades.

The State Government may examine the issue of manufacturing these tools and equipment at the ITIs as a matter of policy, and avoid the purchase of these items from the market. Detailed specifications regarding these items are not given in the list of tools and equipment prescribed. The State Government may, however, adopt the specifications on the basis of similar items already available at the Industrial Training Institutes. It may be mentioned that at certain industrial training institutes, all the facilities for manufacturing these items may not be available. The State Government may, therefore, examine the possibility of having these items manufactured at those ITIs within the state where all the necessary facilities are available. This will not only result in the saving of a considerable expenditure which the State Government may otherwise have to incur for the purchase of additional tools and equipment as well as furniture, but it will also provide an opportunity to trainees to work on actual jobs during the period of their training.

(b) In addition to the manufacture of tools for their own use, the ITIs can also undertake jobs which have training value and are not repetitive in nature, from Public Sector Undertakings, provided this work is commensurate with the needs for training and also after their requirements of necessary tools, etc., have been met.

Raw materials, spare parts accessories, etc., for all outside orders should generally be provided by customers placing the orders.

2.11 METHOD OF TEACHING IN ITIs

1. Weekly Break-up of Syllabus Guidelines/Time-tables for Instructional and Supervisory Staff

A weekly time-table should be chalked out for each instructional and supervisory staff including Group Instructor, Allied Trade Instructor, Vocational Instructors (Theory/Practical, Workshop Science and Calculation and Engineering Drawing) specifying the exact duties they will be expected to carry out on each working day. The aim should be to fully utilize every available hour.

The spare time of the instructional staff when they are not taking theory/practical classes should be utilized in doing the following:

(i) Checking trainees' sessional work
(ii) Filling progress cards of trainees
(iii) Making sectional registers up-to-date
(iv) Preparing charts, drawings, etc., as visual aids
(v) Keeping class progress charts up-to-date
(vi) Chalking out the work plan for the next day
(vii) Maintenance of machines and equipment available in the institute

2. Model Lesson/Demonstrations Plans by Instructional/Supervisory Staff

The senior instructional and supervisory staff of the institute who have undergone a Teachers' Training Course and otherwise considered suitable may conduct model lessons/demonstration classes for the benefit of their instructional staff of the institute.

The principal may arrange one such class every week of about one-hour duration of which 45 minutes or so may be spent on illustrating the proper technique of teaching and the remaining time for group discussion. It is desirable to keep a record of such model lessons and the points arising thereafter during the discussion to spotlight the difficulties felt and remedies suggested as guidance to the staff.

3. Educational Tours by Trainees

The following concessions are admissible to trainees of the Industrial Training Institutes for their educational tours:

(i) For the purpose of obtaining an idea of the actual working conditions, trainees from government and private ITIs nearing completion of their courses may be sent for a week to nearby workshops/ industries.

(ii) The trainee will be entitled to a daily allowance at par with the minimum rates payable to group 'C' employees per day and second-class railway fare for to-and-fro journey.

(DGE&T-12(11)/81-TC, dated 11.6.82)

(iii) Each group of trainees has to be under the charge of a supervisory staff whose absence from the institute will be treated as on duty for the period of the tour.

4. Progress Card for Craftsmen Training Scheme

A progress card should be maintained with respect to every trainee from the date of admission to the institute in a sample proforma in **(Appendix VIII)**.

For awarding sessional marks, monthly tests in all the subjects must be conducted and the performance recorded as usual on a monthly and quarterly basis.

(DGE&T-19(10)/93-CD, dated 21.9.93)

2.12 ADMISSION FOR TRAINING IN ADDITIONAL TRADES

An ex-trainee of an ITI, who is already a National Trade Certificate holder in one of the trades under the Craftsmen Training Scheme, can again seek admission to the ITI, provided he/she fulfills all the conditions regarding educational qualifications, age, etc., prescribed for the purpose of admission to the new trade.

An Instructor with a three-year experience in the trade and with the required skill standard may be allowed to take a test in another (allied) trade with the prior approval of the Director. If he/she passes the test in the allied trade, he/she may be given an advance increment as an incentive. However, only one increment may be allowed to an Instructor even if he/she obtains National Trade Certificates in more than one allied trade.

2.13 WEARING OF UNIFORMS BY TECHNICAL STAFF

For the sake of discipline during practical hours, all gazetted and non-gazetted technical staff at the ITIs should wear a khaki overcoat. Such uniforms will be supplied free of cost to the members of the non-gazetted staff. These would be according to the norms laid down, if any, by the State Government for the supply of similar clothing to other government servants of comparable status.

2.14 GRANTS TO INDUSTRIAL TRAINING INSTITUTES

1. Training Grant

A training grant is allowed to each institute at ₹400/- per month per trainee for engineering trades and ₹300/- per month per trainee for non-engineering trades to cover the cost of the following:

(i) Raw materials
(ii) Consumable stores such as oil, steel, cotton waste, etc.
(iii) Replacement of hand tools
(iv) Repairs to equipment on account of wear and tear
(v) Cost of stationery for training purpose (not for office)
(vi) Cost of light, water and power

(DGE&T-19/15/2007-CD, dated 2.6.2008)

2. Provision for Maintenance of Equipment/Machinery

A provision of maintenance head of 1–3% of the total cost of machines in an ITI in the annual budget every year has to be made. This norm would, however, be applicable to machine tools and related equipment only. For this purpose, principals of ITIs may be delegated full powers for repair and maintenance of machinery, tools and equipment and a separate budget for this should be provided to him. Wherever possible, cooperation from the industry could be sought to overcome neglected machinery problems in ITIs.

(DGE&T-19(3)/89-CD, dated 31.3.89)

3. Adequate Fund Availability for Raw Material

Adequate fund should be provided by State Governments/Union Territories for proper maintenance of equipment and purchase of adequate raw material.

(DGE&T-19(7)/90-CD, dated 25.5.90)

4. Contingent Grant or Contingent Expenditure

(i) Postage stamps/stationary,
(ii) Purchase of government publications,
(iii) Repairs to and washing of workshop clothing,
(iv) Freight,
(v) Mazdoor hire and cartage of stores,
(vi) Miscellaneous expenditure at training institutes, and
(vii) Contingent expenditure at hostels. Contingent expenditure does not cover expenditure on items like rent and taxes in respect of hostels, repairs to building, etc.

5. Technical Books and Magazines

(i) It is necessary for each institute to have technical books, technical magazines and other books related to trades taught at the institute for instructional staff and trainees to refer. For this, expenditure of ₹25/- per month per trainee is allowed.

(ii) The orders prescribing the technical books for libraries at State Directorates and ITIs are circulated by DGE&T from time to time. These books are suggestive ones, and out of these, only those books may be purchased which are technically considered to be of immediate value to the State Directorate.

(iii) Noting that the existing provision of ₹25/- per trainee per month for purchasing technical magazines and books for libraries at ITIs is inadequate for setting up technical libraries on a proper footing, an additional initial expenditure is considered necessary for the purpose.

At the time of establishing a new ITI, initial expenditure for the setting up of a library will be as follows:

(a) For an ITI with seats up to 256 — ₹50,000.00/-
(b) For an ITI with seats more than 256 — ₹1,00,000.00/-

(DGE&T-19(24) /2010-CD, dated 5.10.2010)

(iv) The entire initial expenditure mentioned above involved in the setting up of technical libraries at ITIs shall be utilized for the purchase of technical books only.

6. Sports and Recreation Grant

An expenditure of ₹50/- per trainee per month is allowed for recreation (newspaper, etc.) of trainees.

(DGE&T-19(24) / 2010-CD, dated 5.10.2010)

7. Medical Grant

An expenditure of ₹100/- per trainee per month is allowed to cover the cost of medicines and other requirements of the dispensary at the institute.

(DGE&T-19(24)/2010-CD, dated 5.10.2010)

8. Grant for Stipend

Refer Para 4(viii).

9. Grant for Trade Testing

Refer Chapter 4.

10. Grant for Workshop Clothing

Refer Para 7 on page 26

11. Grant for Travelling Allowance

As per State Government rules

12. Grant for Maintenance of Building, etc. to be provided by State Governments

No fixed scale has been laid down to meet the cost of maintenance of buildings, furniture, rent rates and taxes. This will depend on individual requirement.

2.15 RECORD CARDS OF TRAINEES WHO PASS OUT—FOLLOW UP

(i) The form of the record card to be maintained regarding ex-trainees of ITIs is given in **(Appendix X).**

(ii) Record cards should be maintained to ensure that the passed-out trainees have been able to secure employment. If employed, the name of the employer, etc., should be given, failing which, the whereabouts of the unemployed trainees should be shown in the record cards.

(iii) The instructional staff should be advised to mix with trainees and create confidence in their minds so that they may, after leaving the institute, keep in close touch with the instructors. When the trainees present themselves for receiving the National Trade Certificates, the importance of keeping the principal informed about their future careers must be impressed upon them. They should also be asked to report periodically, say every three months, till they succeed in getting employment. Further, with a view to encourage correspondence by the trainees, they may be permitted to write letters to the instructional staff without having to pay for postage. Such a system is already in vogue in employment exchanges, where free postage cards are issued to the registrants. Similar cards can be issued to trainees who pass out from the institutes.

2.16 CONCESSIONS TO TRAINEES FOR ACTIVE SERVICE IN ARMED FORCES

The following concessions may be made to trainees of ITIs who volunteer for active services in the Indian Armed Forces and are enrolled:

(i) Trainees of ITIs who volunteer for active service in the Indian Armed Forces during National Emergency and are enrolled for such services, may be allowed to discontinue the training at the industrial institutes, without being asked to refund the cost of training, etc.

(ii) On return from active service, if these trainees want to continue their training to complete the course, they may be allowed to do so as though they had not left the training. In the case of scholarship holders, they will be allowed to enjoy the scholarship for the remaining period of their training, subject to the condition that the total period of drawing the scholarship does not exceed 18 months.

(iii) Trainees who are drafted for approved active service in the Indian Armed Forces during a National Emergency within three months before the commencement of their final trade test, may be allowed to appear for the All India Trade Test on their return. This should be subject to the condition that the services rendered by them in the Indian Armed Forces fall in the same trade and the total period, i.e. training at the institute and service in the Indian Armed Forces exceeds 18 months.

2.17 LICENCES FOR MECHANIC (MOTOR VEHICLE) TRAINEES

Driving is included in the syllabus of Mechanical Motor Vehicle trade. However, a driving license may not be required by a trainee undergoing training in an ITI, approved by the Central/State Government, as per notification of Government of India, Ministry of Surface Transport (a copy of the Gazette Notification is at **(Appendix XI)**.

2.18 TIME TABLES FOR INSTRUCTIONAL AND SUPERVISORY STAFF

A weekly time table should be chalked out for each instructional and supervisory staff including Group Instructor, Allied Trade Instructor, Vocational Instructors (Practical), Vocational Instructor (Theory, W/Shop

Science and Calculation and Engineering Drawing) specifying the exact duties they will be expected to carry out on each working day. The aim should be to fully utilize every available hour.

The spare time of the instructional staff when they are not taking theory/practical classes should be utilized in doing the following:

(i) Checking trainees' sessional work
(ii) Filling progress cards of trainees
(iii) Bringing sectional registers up-to-date
(iv) Preparing charts, drawing, etc. as visual aids
(v) Keeping the class progress chart up-to-date
(vi) Chalking out the work plan for next day
(vii) Maintenance of Machines and Equipment available in the institute

2.19 STAFF MEETINGS

One of the regular features of training activities in an Industrial Training Institute should be instructional/supervisory staff meetings at different levels to take stock of the progress made in the training programme, to spell out and discuss difficulties encountered at different levels in implementing the programme and to chalk out the future plan of action.

The principal may hold the meeting of the supervisory and instructional staff, depending upon the size of the institute at regular intervals at least once in a month. Proper record should be kept of the minutes of these monthly meetings and of the decisions arrived at and actions taken. These records should be submitted to the Inspecting Officers. In a small institute having a seating capacity up to 250, these meetings may not be necessary.

2.20 REFERENCE MATERIAL AND TRAINING AID

The following reference material should normally be available in the Institute.

(i) In the Office of the Principal

(a) Layout plan of the institute
(b) Layout plan of the workshop giving locations of machines installed
(c) Layout showing the electrical installation in the workshop
(d) Layout of the electrical distribution in the institute premises
(e) Organizational charts of the institute
(f) Chart showing the up-to-date trade wise number of trainees who have passed their trade test from the institute. (Additional information of the number of passed-out trainees who have secured employment or settled down may also be displayed wherever available.)
(g) Duty charts of instructional/supervisory staff
(h) Weekly time-table of each section

(ii) In the Workshop Sections

(a) Section layout plan showing position of the machines installed, their specifications, individual and total connected load
(b) Prescribed syllabus and standard tools and equipment list for the trade
(c) Charts showing the break-up of syllabus on week wise/month wise basis

(d) Weekly time table of the section
(e) Section progress card, showing practical exercises completed by trainees individually
(f) Visual aids, charts, drawing and models (this will also include drawing of each type of machine installed in the section, showing its parts and special features)
(g) Instructions on the maintenance of machines and equipment
(h) Chart showing safety rules to be observed in the section
(i) First-aid instructions

2.21 INTERNAL INSPECTION OF INSTITUTES

Regular internal inspections of the institute may be carried for ensuring smooth working of the training programme and to increase efficiency of the administration.

(i) Internal inspections of Institute may be carried out at two different levels:
  (a) Group instructor's
  (b) Principal's

  These inspections are confined to one section at one time and be intensively covering all aspects of the activities of the section and factors affecting the training programme.
(ii) The inspection date will normally be fixed in advance and the section will be informed of the date.
(iii) The Principal will normally spend two hours in the section under inspection and the inspections will be done on four days per week preferably.
(iv) In institutes where it may not be possible for the Principal to inspect all the sections of the institute due to administrative reasons, the Group Instructor may carry out inspections. In that case, inspections may be so arranged that the Principal and the Group Instructor may inspect the different sections during their consecutive inspections.
(v) Proper record should be kept of these inspections, deficiencies observed and remedies suggested to remove them may be noted. Action taken on these suggestions should also be checked and recorded at the time of the next inspection.

2.22 DEVELOPMENT OF INSTRUCTIONAL MATERIALS TO IMPROVE QUALITY OF TRAINING

(i) The State Government should set up media resource centres and effort should be made to develop instructional material in the local languages. **(DGE&T 29 (2)/87-CD, dated 3.4.87)**
(ii) State Directors and UT Administrators dealing with the CTS may encourage the instructional staff of ITIs located in their states to develop suitable training materials in English or a regional languages. The producers of very good materials may be rewarded at the rate of ₹1000/- per material (a book, a model, set of charts, transparencies and slides, etc.).

(DGE&T 29(5)/87 CD, dated 6.5.87)

2.23 MANAGEMENT INFORMATION SYSTEM

Management Information System is to be established both at the State HQ and the regional HQ of big states for a good networking between the State Training Directorates, Industries and the DGE&T to facilitate the planning and decision making, both at state and national levels. For bigger states, similar Management Information System may be established at regional HQ of the state.

2.24 STATISTICAL RETURNS PERTAINING TO CRAFTSMEN TRAINING SCHEME

(i) Four statistical returns proforma pertaining to Craftsmen Training Scheme as prescribed viz TS-1,TS-2, TS-3 and TS-4. The statistical returns prescribed are required to be sent annually by the ITIs to DGE&T, New Delhi, through State Directors. State Directors may send the consolidated return to DGE&T in respect of ITIs in their state. The information in respect of government as well as private institutes may be sent separately and the same proformae should be used for the purpose.

A set of these proformae is given in **(Appendix XVII)** (TS-1), **(Appendix XVIII)** (TS-2), **(Appendix XIX)** (TS-3) and **(Appendix XX)** (TS-4). The information as per these proformae may kindly be sent to the statistical section (Training), DGE&T, Ministry of Labour & Employment , 2-A/3 Kundan Mansion, Asaf Ali Road, New Delhi 110 002.

(DGET-14(6)/87-TC, dated 31.1.91)

(ii) State Directors may send the computerized returns in respect of Craftsmen Training Scheme. The return should include details like trainees admitted, passed out trainees, their placement, drop-outs and certificates to be issued.

(DGE&T-19(18)/96-CD, dated 30.4.97)

2.25 INSPECTION OF INDUSTRIAL TRAINING INSTITUTES

(i) The Inspecting Officer of the State Directorate of Training should visit the training institutes under their charge as frequently as possible and inspect and advise on the training and the work of the trainees. They should conduct trade tests for the trainees from time to time, check the efficiency of the instructors and assist Principals of training institutes in all matters relating to the training classes.

(ii) The decisions of the National Council for Vocational Training on the subject of inspection of training institutes are reproduced below:

(a) Each training centre in the state should be inspected at least once a quarter by an Inspecting Officer of the State Directorate of Training.

(b) Beside, at least one centre in the state should be inspected once a year by a tripartite term consisting of

- State Director-in-charge of Training;
- representative of industries who are running training schemes of their own; and
- a representative of the labour organization.

(c) A few selected centres of the each state should be inspected once a year by the officers of the Training Directorate of the Directorate General of Employment & Training of Ministry of Labour & Employment

(d) Regional officers should be appointed to assist the State Councils and the Central Government in formulating new proposals and carrying out the policies of the Central Government and the National Council and to carry out detailed inspection of each centre at least once a year on behalf of the National Council.

(iii) The inspection questionnaire is given at **(Appendix XV)**.

(iv) One of the functions of the National Council for Vocational Training is to arrange for ad-hoc or periodical inspection of training institutions in the country to ensure that the standards prescribed by the Council are being followed. This will be exercised through the Directorate of Training, Ministry of Labour. Training institutes shall afford all facilities for inspection to the staff of the Directorate of Training, Ministry of Labour, or any member of an examining body set by the National Council for Vocational Training or any member of a committee appointed by the National Council.

(v) The requisite information regarding inspections carried out may be furnished biannually in the proforma attached **(Appendix XVI)** so that the information relating to the half-year ending 30th June and 31st December is received by the Directorate General of Employment and Training (Statistical Section) by the end of the month following the period under review. If the return is not received from any State Government, it will be assumed that no inspection has been carried out.

(vi) (a) Every year a team of inspecting officers from the Directorate General of Employment and Training will select as many centres as possible for inspection in each State.

(b) The State Directors will select as many centres as possible for inspection in each state.

- At the conclusion of these inspections, a seminar will be organized by the State Directors wherein the Principals and the inspecting officers of the Directorate General of Employment and Training will participate. Non-official members, particularly industrialists who have participated in tripartite inspections may also be invited in the seminar. The final report by the tripartite team will be discussed in the seminars.
- The deliberations and the report of this seminar along with the major deficiencies and defects noticed and recommendations for removal will be brought to the notice of the Director of Training, Directorate General of Employment and Training, and followed up in this Directorate for early removal of the deficiencies noticed.
- In addition to the above, a seminar may be held at the state level at the State Directorate wherein all the Principals of the industrial training institutes in the state, officers of the State Directorate and other concerned will participate. Such a seminar should be held once in a year and preferably about two months before the meeting of the State Government representatives concerned with training schemes.
- The object of the seminars at the state level will be to discuss the administrative as well as technical matters relating to the implementation of the training schemes at the state level whereas the object of the seminars as are held at present is to discuss the discrepancies noticed during the inspections and the methods for improvement.

(b) The Director of Training will organize a proper plan of inspection of the training centres by the officers of the Directorate and intimate this to the directors at least two months in advance so as to enable them to plan tripartite inspections and seminars.

(c) A number of States have enquired as to what should be the proforma for reports of the tripartite teams. This matter has been carefully considered and it has been felt that while the tripartite teams may not be tied down to furnish their reports of inspection of industrial training institutes in a prescribed proforma, the reports of the tripartite teams should, however, reflect the general picture of the institute. The members of such a team may be informed accordingly and requested also to embody the information in their reports on the following specific matters:

- (i) the training arrangements in the industrial training institutes specially in regard to the methods adopted and the arrangements for training;
  (ii) the adequacy or otherwise of the machine tools and equipment provided for training;
  (iii) the general calibre of the instructors in regard to their knowledge of the theory and practice of the craft; and
  (iv) the discipline of the trainees.
- Whether the training imparted is up to the standard and skill obtained is as per the need of the industry.
- Any suggestion for improvement.

With a view to ensure the minimum standard of training prescribed by the NCVT, two inspections of the ITIs should be carried out every year, one by the state and one by the

DGE&T on a zonal basis. The DGE&T will carry out only technical inspection and the State Government/Union Territory administrations should do administrative inspections of the ITIs.

It is required that in future a statement showing the action taken and/or proposed to be taken by the State Directorate, etc., to remove the defects and shortcomings may kindly be attached with each inspection report when forwarded to the Ministry.

It will be appreciated that the above suggestion will reduce the correspondence in this connection to a considerable extent from both sides and will also enable the State Directors to review at the end of each month the progress of remedial action taken on each inspection.

The inspections of the industrial institutes would require a close follow-up of the training programmes in order to ensure that the training curriculum adopted for each trade is in conformity with the prescribed syllabus and the desired proficiencies are attained by the trainees without running the risk of wastage due to failures at the conclusion of the course. To achieve the above objective, the programme of inspecting the ITIs would have to be intensified. The Technical Officer of the State Directorate according to the recommendations of the State Representatives in their seventh meeting held on 8th and 9th October, 1964, would inspect every ITI twice in a year. During these inspections, their officers would concentrate on the technical and academic aspects of training and would offer their concrete and positive suggestions on the improvement of the standard of training.

2.26 TRAINING IN DUAL TRADES

There is no objection to an ex-trainee of an ITI who is already a National Trade Certificate holder in one of the trades under the Craftsmen Training Scheme, being admitted to the ITI, provided he/she fulfills all the conditions regarding educational qualifications, age, etc., prescribed for the purpose of admission to the new trade.

On the recommendation of the representatives of states at their sixth meeting vide Item 15, it has been decided that an Instructor with three years' experience in the trade and with the required standard of skill may be allowed to take a test in another (allied) trade with the previous approval of the Director. If he/she passes the test in the allied trade, he/she may be given an advance increment as an incentive. However, only one increment may be allowed to an Instructor even if he/she obtains National Trade Certificate in more than one allied trade.

2.27 DEFINITION OF TECHNICAL STAFF

Decided that the terms of technical staff "occurring" in Letter TC/TP-3/96/63, dated 17.4.1964 covers the Drawing, Mathematics and Language Instructors and also trade instructors in both engineering as well as non-engineering trades at the Industrial Training Institutes.

2.28 TRAINING IN INDUSTRY

Members of the technical staff of Industrial Training Institutes in all engineering trades should be deputed to industry for industrial experience and/or refresher training in accordance with the scheme forwarded with Letter TP-3(102)/63, dated 26.11.1963 subject to the condition that not more than one member is deputed from an Industrial Training Institute at a time and not more than once in five years unless new equipment or process on which training is essential are involved. Normal duration of such training should be one month. Prior approval of the programme of training by the DGE&T is not necessary.

2.29 SETTING UP OF A PERFORMANCE APPRAISAL SYSTEM AND SYSTEMATIC IDENTIFICATION OF STAFF TRAINING NEEDS

(i) Each State Directorate may work out a concrete training plan for each ITI based upon the self-appraisal of individual instructors supported by his/her supervisors. Principals of ITIs may be delegated with the financial powers to depute instructors for training at least for the courses where no fees has been prescribed and only TA/DA are required to be paid to the staff. Ad-hoc appointments may be made in place of instructors deputed for training/retraining.

(DGE&T-19(17)/96-CD, dated 27.5.1997)

(ii) Each State Directorate may appointment of 20% more instructors in ITIs as training reserves apart from existing norms of one instructor per trade/unit so that they could be deputed for training on regular basis without affecting the regular training programme of the institute. However, additional requirement of 20% would not be insisted at the time of SCIR.

(DGE&T-19(9)/2008-CD, dated 15.12.2008)

The State Directors should take up the proposal for ad-hoc appointment/training reserves with their respective Finance Department for approval.

2.30 CONCESSIONS TO TRAINEES FOR ACTIVE SERVICE IN ARMED FORCES

The following concessions may be made to trainees of the Industrial Training Institutes who volunteer for active services in the Indian Armed Forces and are enrolled:

(i) Trainees of the Industrial Training Institutes who volunteer for active service in the Indian Armed Forces during National Emergency and are enrolled for such services, may be allowed to discontinue the training at the Industrial Training Institutes, without being asked to refund the cost of training, etc.

(ii) On return from active service, if these trainees want to continue their training to complete the course, they may be allowed to do so as though they had not left the training. In the case of scholarship holders, they will be allowed to enjoy the scholarship for the remaining period of their training, subject to the condition that the total period of drawing scholarship does not exceed 18 months.

(iii) Trainees who are drafted for approved active service in the Indian Armed Forces during a National Emergency, within three months before the commencement of their final trade test may be allowed to appear for All India Trade Test on their return, provided the services rendered by them in the Indian Armed Forces is in the same trade and the total period, i.e. training at the institute and service in the Indian Armed Forces exceeds 18 months.

Chapter 3

Manpower Requirement, Role and Responsibilities

3.1 ORGANIZATION CHART AND ADMINISTRATION OF ITIs

Organization Chart of an Industrial Training Institute may be followed as per **(Appendix VI)**.

3.2 STAFF ADMISSIBLE FOR INDUSTRIAL TRAINING INSTITUTES

1. Administrative Set-Up of an ITI

Technical Staff

S. No. 1	Name of Post 2	Basic, namely seating capacity of the Institute 3	No. of Posts Admissible 4
1.	Principal (Sr. Scale) Vice-Principal (of the rank of Class II Principal and posts interchangeable)	ITIs with 1000 and above seats	1 2
2.	Principal (Sr. Scale)	ITIs with 600 to 999 seats	1
3.	Principal (Sr. Scale)	ITIs with 400 to 599 seats	1
4.	Principal (Jr. Scale)	ITIs up to 399 seats	1
5.	Superintendent (non-gazetted)	ITIs below 200 seats	1
6.	Group Instructor (formerly called Foreman)	(i) No GI for ITI with capacity lees then 8 units (ii) For Every eight Units or more than 8 units and in multiplication of 8 units	1
7.	Vocational/Craft Instructor	For two trade unit	2, One VI must be with Diploma/Degree qualification
8.	Training and Placement Officer (in the rank of Deputy Director/Joint Director)	Having 1000 or more sanctioned seats	(i) A post of Training and Placement Officer at each Regional Centre under Central and State Governments.

(Contd.)

S. No. 1	Name of Post 2	Basic, namely seating capacity of the Institute 3	No. of Posts Admissible 4
			(ii) One such post to be created in an ITI having 1000 or more sanctioned seats (iii) Other institutes having less than 1000 seats, a staff member of appropriate level should be entrusted to carry out the function of liaison with industry **(DGE&T-19(6)/90-CD, dated 15.05.90)**
9.	Drawing Instructor		One for 144 (Engineering) seats sanctioned Additional instructor will be required on increase in every 144 trainees. upto 144 Engineers seats – one instructor **(DGE&T-19(4)/2013-CD dated 26th June, 2013)**
10.	Mathematics Instructor		One for 144 engineering seats sanctioned **(DGE&T-12(20)/81-TC, dated 08.06.81)**
11.	Allied Trade Instructor		The post of Allied Trade Instructor may not be provided in the ITIs in which allied trade training could be carried out by the respective trade instructor. However, the existing staff on all such posts may be phased out gradually. In case of new institutes the post of Allied Instructor is not required. **(DGE&T-19(8)/89-CD, dated 31.3.89)** **(DGE&T-19(4)/2013-CD dated 26th June, 2013)**
12.	(i) Mechanic Machine Tool Maintenance		One when six units exist in an ITI in the following trades: Machinist, Turner, Tool and Die Maker, Instrument Mechanic. Not mandatory can be out-sourced.
	- do -		One in each ITI working in three shifts and having trades of Machinist and/or Turner if Mill Wrights are otherwise not admissible. Not mandatory can be out-sourced.
	- do -		One to be attached to an ITI with 600 seats or more or to the State Directorate, if there is no such ITI. Not mandatory can be out-sourced.
	(ii) Maintenance Mechanic for Maintenance Section		(ii) One for 15-30 of equivalent machines. Two for 30-60 equivalent machines. Three for 60-90 equivalent machines and above. The M/W and Maintenance Mechanic already appointed under the existing pattern to be taken into account and only one maintenance mechanic to be appointed for the present where three or less Maintenance Mechanics are admissible. Not mandatory can be out-sourced.

(*Contd.*)

S. No. 1	Name of Post 2	Basic, namely seating capacity of the Institute 3	No. of Posts Admissible 4
13.	Carpenter		One at each such Industrial Training Institute where the number of seats sanctioned is 250 or more and where the post of Instructor Carpentry does not exist. *However the said post not required in new institues may be out sourced.
14.	Motor Driving Instructor		One for Mechanic (Motor Vehicle) trade
15.	Employability Skills Instructor		*One full time instructor is required for 1000 seats & above. For seats less than 1000, the instructor can be out sourced/on contract basis.
16.	Stenography Instructor (English)		One for each unit.
17.	Language Instructor (English)		One for each ITI where the Trade of Stenography (English) exists.
18.	Stenography Instructor (Hindi)		One for each unit.
19.	Language Instructor (Hindi)		One for each ITI where the trade of Stenography (Hindi) exists.

*(DGE&T 19 (4)/2013-CD dated 26 June 2013)

(i) MINISTERIAL (CLASS III) AND CLASS IV STAFF to be decided by the respective State Directorate.

Sanctioned Strength	Clerks		Workshop Attendants	Peons and Malis	Safaiwala	Chowkidars
	UDC	LDC				
For a minimum of 50 seats	1	—	1	1	1	1
For a minimum of 100 seats	2	1	2	2	1	2
For a minimum of 150 seats	2	2	2	3	2	3
For a minimum of 200 seats	3	2	3	3	2	3
For a minimum of 250 seats	3	3	3	4	3	4

Remarks: Above the sanctioned strength of 250 seats, for every 50 to 100 additional seats, one additional Clerk, UD or LD according to the circumstances, one Workshop Attendant and one Class IV staff may be provided.

Where the number of Clerks is at least three, one of them may be appointed as Head Clerk.

Where the number of Clerks is six or more, one Office Superintendent may be appointed.

(ii) Hostel Staff

(a) Hostel Superintendent-cum-Physical Training Instructor cum Contractor of The institute — One for the hostel attached to each institute

(b) Hostel Clerk — UDC or LDC, one for each hostel, where the actual strength is 50 or more in addition to the Hostel Superintendent.

(c) Hostel Class IV Staff to be decided by respective State Directorate on need basis.

No. of Trainees in the Hostel	Safaiwala	Chowkidars
1 to 50 trainees	1	1
51 to 100 trainees	2	2
101 to 200 trainees	3	4

For every additional 100 trainees in the hostel, one extra chawkidar and one extra Sweeper may be provided.

(iii) Medical Staff

(a) Medical Officer
(b) Compounder
(c) Dresser

First Aid facility need to be made available in the institute. It may be outsourced as per requirement. Tie-up with doctor/clinic/hospital is mandatory.

The norms at (i) and (ii) above have revised and New ITIs may appoint supporting staff (Ministerial staff like clerk) head clerk, Accountant, superintendent, multi skill persons & hostel staff may be allowed to be employed on contract basis/out sourced & may be need based.

DGE&T 19 (4)/2013-CD dated 26-6-13

1. Storekeepers

(i) Institutes with less than 250 seats — One Storekeeper
(ii) Institutes with 251 to 599 seats — One Storekeeper and one Asst. Storekeeper
(iii) Institutes with 600 to 899 seats — One Storekeeper and two Asst. Storekeepers
(iv) Institutes with 900 seats and above — One Store Superintendent and three Asst. Storekeepers

The scales of pay of the Store Superintendent, Storekeepers and Asst. Storekeepers will be according to the state's scales of pay for such posts in other departments of the State Government.

2. Librarian One Librarian for an institute with 400 or more seats is recommended.

(DGE&T-29(3)/86-CD, dated 17.02.86)

3. Switchboard Attendant Where there is a separate electric sub-station at the institutes and no attendant is provided by PWD, one sub-station attendant for each shift could be appointed. The scale of pay of the attendant will be according to the state's scale. For new institutes the Switch Board attendant may be outsourced as required

4. Accountant One Accountant should be provided in each institute.

5. Electrician One in each ITI where Electrician trade does not exist. For new ITIs Electrical maintenance work of institute may be out sourced/contract basis where the Electrician trade does not exist.

6. Substitute They are admissible in respect of those instructors sent for training at CTI/ATIs.

2. Qualification, Experience and Method of Direct Recruitment and Promotion of Technical Staff at Industrial Training Institutes

Sl. No.	Name of Post and its Status	Capacity of ITI	Qualifications	Mode of recruitment
1.	Principal (Sr. Scale) (equivalent to Executive Engineer of the state)	For institutes with 400 seats and above	*For Direct Recruitment* A degree in the appropriate branch of Engineering/Technology of a recognized University or equivalent with 5 years' experience. Or Diploma in the appropriate branch of Engineering/Technology from a recognized board/institution or equivalent with eight years' experience in a workshop or factory or concern of repute engaged in production or in teaching in a recognized institution. *For Promotees:* In accordance with the existing rules of the states.	Promotion 100%
2.	Principal (Jr. Scale)/ Vice-Principal (equivalent to Asstt. Executive Engineer of the state)	In the case of ITIs with seating capacity below 400 seats But in the case of ITIs with more than 400 seats, a Vice-Principal to assist the Principal would have to be appointed at the rate of one Vice-Principal for every additional 300 seats or part thereof.	*For direct recruitment:* A degree in the appropriate branch of Engineering/Technology from a recognized board/institution or university or equivalent with 5 years' experience. **Or** Diploma in the appropriate branch of Engineering/Technology from a recognised board/institution or equivalent with eight years' experience in a workshop or factory or concern of repute engaged in production or in teaching in a recognized institution. *For Promotees:* In accordance with the existing rules of the states.	Direct: 50% Promotion: 50%
3.	Superintendent (non-gazetted)	For institute below 200 seats	Same as for Group Instructors	Promotion: 100% Direct recruitment will be resorted to only if none of the instructors is considered suitable for promotion.
4.	Group instructor (formerly called Foreman)	One for every eight units	(a) Matric or equivalent (b) Diploma in Technology/Engineering (c) Five years practical experience in a reputed Industrial concern or in a training institute	25% by direct; 75% by promotion
5.	Vocational Instructor/ Craft Instructor		**Academic**: 10th class pass or its equivalent **Technical**: Degree in appropriate branch of Engineering from recognized university or equivalent. **Or** Three year Diploma in the appropriate branch of Engineering from recognized board/institute or equivalent **Or**	

(*Contd.*)

Sl. No.	Name of Post and its Status	Capacity of ITI	Qualifications	Mode of recruitment
			National Apprenticeship Certificate (NAC) in relevant Trade **Or** National Trade Certificate (NTC) in relevant Trade. **Practical Experience** in an Industry of Training/Teaching Institutes—One Year for Degree Holder Two Years for Diploma Holder Three Years for NAC/NTC **(DGE&T-19(8)/2008-CD, dated 23.12.2008)**	
6.	Motor Driver		The Motor Driver, admissible at the ITIs where Motor Mechanic trade is in operation, should possess a license in heavy vehicle driving.	
7.	Vocational Instructor: One VI for a Workshop Calculation and Science, and Engineering Drawing (Engineering Trades)	One Vocational Instructor for a minimum of 36 trainees failing under the same group of trades.	(a) Academic: Passed 10th standard examination under 10+2 system of education. (b) **Technical:** Passed degree or three years diploma in appropriate branch of Engineering from a recognized institute. (c) Possesses certificate under Craft Instructor Training Scheme (One Year Course) or should have successfully completed minimum two modules, viz., Teaching Methodology Module (three month duration) and Trades Technology modules (three months duration) under Craftsmen Instructor Training Programme on modular pattern or should have passed a one-year course from a Technical Teacher Training Institute (TTTI) under Ministry of Human Resource Development.	
8.	Stenography Instructor		(a) Matriculation or equivalent (b) Five years' experience as Stenographer with at least a speed of 120 words per minute in shorthand and 40 words per minute in typing. (c) Good knowledge of English and proficiency in the language (Hindi in case of Hindi Stenography)	
9.	Language Instructor for Stenography		Trained graduate, preferably with a masters or an honours degree in English/Hindi **Essential:**	
10.	Mechanic Machine Tool Maintenance		(a) Matric or equivalent (b) Diploma in Engineering or technology or a Certificate of apprenticeship from an industrial undertaking of repute only in one of trades of Fitter, Turner, Machinist (Grinder) and Machinist. (c) Five years' of experience in the repair and Maintenance of machines in an industrial organization of repute. ***Desirable***: Administrative and organizing ability	
11.	Employability Skills Instructors		BBA with two years experience or MBA.	

(Contd.)

Sl. No.	Name of Post and its Status	Capacity of ITI	Qualifications	Mode of recruitment
12.	Computer Instructor		Graduate in Engineering **or** Graduate in Computer Science with atleast 1 year experience **or** Diploma in Computer Engineering with 2 years experience **or** NTC/NAC in COPA with 3 years experience. The experience should be in a reputed Industrial concern or in a training Institute. **DGE&T-19(4)/2013-CD dated 26/6/2013**	

NOTES

I. (i) There should be the same cadres as per apprenticeship groups to the Group Instructor level (i.e. they will be appointed/promoted within these groups.

(ii) A certificate holder will rise to the post of Group Instructor.

(iii) For promotion, two years' of minimum experience in the immediately preceding post is necessary.

II. The posts carrying the same scale of pay at the ITIs and the State Directorate of Training should be declared interchangeable in the interest of administrative convenience.

III. The technical officers at the State Headquarters should be in the ratio of *75% of Mechanical and 25% Electrical /Automobile, depending on the workload.*

3. Norms/Qualifications of Instructor for Multi-Skill Courses

The following norms are to be followed for appointment of Instructor for Broad Based Basic Training:

(i) For 6 Modules of BBBT: Six Vocational Instructors (VIs), one each for 6 modules of relevant trades qualifications of VI should be as per para 2 above

(ii) For Workshop Calculation Science and Engineering Drawing: One Vocational Instructor having diploma in relevant field

(iii) For Generic Module: One contract/part-time/guest faculty

The following norms are to be followed for appointment of Instructor for Advanced Module

One instructor of the following qualification for each advanced module in the sector

(i) *Degree in relevant branch of Engineering with a minimum of three years of teaching/industrial experience in the relevant field

OR

(ii) *Diploma in relevant branch of Engineering with a minimum of five years of teaching/industrial experience in the relevant field

OR

(iii) Higher National Trade Certificate (HNTC) in related area with minimum of five years of teaching/ industrial experience in the relevant field.

*Detailed qualification for instructors is given in the syllabi of BBBT and advanced module of each sector.

4. Honorarium for Guest Instructors

Honorarium for guest lecturers for the basic courses under the Craftsmen Training Scheme will be ₹200.00 for first hour and ₹150.00 for subsequent hours subject to a ceiling of 3 hours per day and 50 hours per month.

[DGE&T-12/04/ 2005-CD, dated 27.12.2005]

For a session of three hours for advanced level course; ₹800/-

(DGE&T-19(16)/2007-CD, dated 2.6. 2008)

5. Salaries to be paid to the Staff Being Engaged by Private ITIs

A minimum of $2/3^{rd}$ of the salary being paid to a government servant of equivalent level should be paid to the faculty/staff members of the private ITIs. **(DGE&T 19(19)/95–CD, dated 16.8.1996)**

6. Qualifications for Post of Technical Assistant at Headquarters of State Directorates of Training

Name of the Post	Minimum Educational Qualifications	Technical Qualifications
Technical Assistant	Matriculation or equivalent	***Essential***
		(a) A diploma in mechanical engineering
		(b) Industrial experience of three years which may include teaching experience up to two years
		Desirable
		1. A certificate of proficiency in a mechanical engineering trade with five years of industrial experience, part of which may be spent in teaching
		2. Ability to supervise the work of others
Scale of pay: State scale of pay for comparative posts		State scale of pay for comparative posts.

NOTE: It has been observed in certain cases that the qualifications for the post of principals of the industrial training institutes, technical staff at headquarters of the training directorates and apprenticeship and assistant apprenticeship advisers are being applied to the existing staff also. The qualifications are not to be applied in the case of those who have already been officiating in their present posts for three years or more. The State Government/administrations are, therefore, requested to keep in view the decision quoted above while framing recruitment rules with respect to the posts in question for making appointments, promotions, etc., thereto.

7. Qualifications Prescribed for Hostel Superintendent-cum-Physical Training Instructor/Caretaker

(i) Graduate or equivalent
(ii) Organizing and administrative ability
(iii) Ability to keep and maintain proper accounts of expenditure
(iv) Ability to supervise games and sports and other recreational facilities
(v) A certificate in physical education

These need not be insisted upon in the case of existing incumbents of the posts.

8. Qualifications for Technical Staff at State Headquarters

Sl. No.	Post	Qualifications
1.	Deputy Director of Training	***Essential***
		Degree/diploma in mechanical/electrical/automobile engineering of a recognized university or an equivalent qualification.

(Contd.)

Sl. No.	Post	Qualifications
		Desirable
		(i) About five years of industrial experience subsequent to graduation in a supervisory capacity in a workshop engaged in production.
		(ii) Some teaching experience in a recognized institute in addition to the above essential qualifications will be desirable.
		(iii) Organizing capacity and administrative ability.
2.	Assistant Director of Training/Inspector of Training	***Essential:*** Degree/diploma in mechanical/electrical/automobile engineering of a recognized university or an equivalent qualification.
		Desirable
		(i) About three years industrial experience subsequent to graduation in a supervisory capacity in a workshop engaged in production.
		(ii) Some teaching experience in a recognized institute in addition to the above essential qualifications will be desirable.
		(iii) Organizing capacity and administrative ability.
		Alternative qualifications:
		A diploma in mechanical/electrical/automobile engineering of a recognized university or an equivalent qualification. *Desirable:*
		(i) About seven years of industrial experience in a supervisory capacity in a workshop engaged in production subsequent to passing diploma. Some teaching experience in a recognized technical institute in addition to the above essential qualifications will be desirable.
		(ii) Organizing capacity and administrative ability.

Mechanical/Electrical/Automobile engineers should be in the ratio of 75% mechanical and 25% in electrical/automobile depending upon the workload.

NOTE: The qualifications suggested are based on the Central Government's recruitment rules. The states may, however, follow their own recruitment rules in this regard.

9. Suggested Duties of Principal, Supervisory and Instructional Staff of Industrial Training Institutes

(i) Principal

The Principal should ensure that:

(a) all the instructions issued to him/her by the higher authorities are properly and expeditiously carried out;

(b) accounts are maintained properly, stores are properly accounted for and verified periodically, and the purchases are according to specification and in good condition;

(c) training programmes are carried out according to schemes;

(d) raw materials are purchased in time and duly supplied;

(e) machine and equipment are properly maintained;

(f) manufactured products are properly accounted for and disposed of in accordance with the rules and instructions issued from time to time;

(g) ensure that the foremen and supervisors maintain an extremely close supervision on the work of instructors and the progress of the classes;

(h) proper discipline is maintained in the institute;

(i) there is close relationship between the trainees and the instructional staff;
(j) proper follow-up is maintained of the passed out trainees;
(k) proper security arrangements are maintained and safety precautions observed;
(l) trainees get the proper medical aid and welfare arrangements are available;
(m) proper facilities to the inspection staff of the State Directorate, DGE&T, and other authorised bodies are provided, and
(n) any other additional duties assigned to the Principal of ITI.

(ii) Group Instructor

The Group Instructors should ensure that

(a) proper coordination is maintained in all the sections and the training programme is carried out efficiently, by personal close check and inspections;
(b) the tests are regularly carried out, the trainees' work is correctly assessed, and proper record is kept in the progress cards;
(c) raw material requirements of the sections are prepared well in advance to enable supply to be arranged in time;
(d) safety precautions are observed in the workshop;
(e) sections function strictly according to the time schedule laid down and proper discipline maintained; and
(f) any other additional duties assigned by the Principal of ITI.

The Group Instructor will also conduct model lessons in his/her own or connected subjects.

The Group Instructor will also carry out any additional work entrusted to him/her by the Principal of the ITI.

Note:

(i) The lessons prepared by the instructors should be checked by the concerned Group Instructor for correct planning and accuracy. This may be done in the beginning of each working day for which the Group Instructor may spend about 15 minutes in each section.
(ii) The Group Instructor may also carry out a check of a certain percentage of these lessons to ensure proper planning of lessons and right standard.
(iii) The Group Instructor will also attend these lectures from time to time to ensure that the proper teaching technique is followed.

(iii) Hostel Superintendent-Cum-Physical Training Instructors

They will be responsible for

1. imparting physical training to the trainees;
2. arranging such cultural activities as are considered essential for creating team spirit, responsibility and sense of discipline amongst the trainees; and
3. any other additional duties assigned by the Principal of ITI.

(iv) Vocational Instructors

The instructors will be responsible for

(a) taking of classes in theory and practice according to the prescribed syllabus and graded exercises;
(b) maintenance of attendance register, progress cards, raw-material register, tool and equipment register, manufacturing register and other sectional records in accordance with the instructions;
(c) checking and correcting of theory notes, practical work and journals of trainees;
(d) preparing charts, drawing and other visual aid material for the section;
(e) ensuring that the machines in the section are in good working condition and are properly cleaned at the closing time daily;

(f) requisitioning of tools and raw materials required for the section;
(g) ensuring close relationship with the trainees;
(h) attending to leave applications of trainees; and
(i) any other additional duties assigned by the Principal of ITI.

Notes:

(i) In giving theoretical training, the instructor will not depend on the textbooks or his/her old notes. He/She will prepare lessons for each lecture and use the current technique of teaching as per the Instruction material for trainers.
(ii) The instructor will check the conditions of tools and equipment in his/her section and will see that the machines are in good working condition before beginning the practical class.

(v) Mechanic Machine Tool Maintenance

The responsibilities include

(a) training all Mechanic Machine Tool Maintenance Instructors who are responsible for the maintenance and repairs of the machinery in all Industrial Training Institutes in the State/Union Territory; and
(b) carrying out special periodical inspection of the machinery in the Industrial Training Institutes in the State/Union Territory and report on the state of maintenance and also to render advise with a view to improve the maintenance.
(c) While Mechanic Machine Tool Maintenance Instructors concerned at the Industrial Training Institutes are responsible for the maintenance and normal repairs of the machinery, the Mechanic Machine Tool Maintenance Instructor will undertake major repairs to the machinery in abnormal cases with the help of the Mechanic Machine Tool Maintenance Instructor concerned.
(d) Any other additional duties assigned by the Principal of ITI.

(DGE&T-2(2)/99-CD, dated 3.6.99

(vi) Training and Placement Cell

Placement Cells need to be set up in every ITI with the following functions, to help the graduates in getting placed in different industries:

(a) Maintaining details of each and every trainee graduating from an ITI with his/her name, address, educational qualification, technical qualification, telephone number, mobile phone number, etc.
(b) Campus selections may be organized by these Placement Cells so that any industry wanting to recruit persons with requisite skills may do so.
(c) Industry should function in close coordination and should give all its requirement of skilled work-force so that any desirous candidate could apply to the concerned industry to seek gainful employment.
(d) These cells should also provide counseling and guidance to the trainees by professionals and experts.
(e) These Placement Cells should also keep track of these graduates until they are suitably employed or for at least three years after completing the training from that institute.
(f) State Government/private bodies would provide appropriate infrastructure including one hall computer with Internet facilities, phone line and fax machine, proper staff including one officer for functioning of these Placement Cells.
(g) Any other additional duties assigned by the Principal of ITI.

(DGE&T-19(28)/2007-CD, dated 2.6.2008)

(vii) Training and Placement Officer

In the new education policy, the Government of India has laid great stress on linkages with the industry for training and placement. In this context, it becomes very essential to have a proper system of selection and placement of trainees in close coordination with industry. In order to accomplish this task systematically and effectively it is felt necessary to have a 'training and placement officer' at each regional centre in each State/ UT and at each RDAT, Ministry of Labour with adequate supporting staff to look after the following activities:

(a) Conducting selection tests and interviews of ITI passed candidates for recruitment at ITIs, in coordination with industrial establishments.

(b) Conducting selection tests and interviews of ITI pass candidates for placement as apprentices under the Apprenticeship Act 1961 at various industrial establishments.

(c) Liaison between ITIs, State Directorates, Industrial establishment and Apprenticeship Advisors (State and Central both) for manpower requirements and placements of ex-trainees in suitable vacancies. With steadily increasing number of Industrial Training Institutes and industrial training establishment under Apprenticeship Training scheme, the above activities are becoming more voluminous and may be properly looked into.

(d) Any other additional duties assigned by the Principal of ITI.

10. Internal Inspection of Institutes

Regular internal inspections of the institute may be carried for ensuring smooth working of the training programme and to increase efficiency of the administration.

(i) Internal inspections of Institute may be carried out at two different levels:

  (a) Group instructor's

  (b) Principal's

These inspections be confined to one section at one time and be intensive and thorough, covering all aspects of the activities of the section and factors affecting the training programme.

(ii) The inspection date will normally be fixed in advance and the section will be informed of the date.

(iii) The Principal will normally spend two hours in the section under inspection and the inspections will be done on four days per week preferably.

(iv) In institutes where it may not be possible for the Principal to inspect all the sections of the institute due to administrative reasons, the Group Instructor may carry out inspections. In that case, inspections may be so arranged that the Principal and the Group Instructor may inspect the different sections during their consecutive inspections.

(v) Proper record should be kept of these inspections. The deficiencies observed and remedies suggested to remove them may be noted. The action taken on these suggestions should also be checked and recorded at the time of the next inspection.

Chapter 4

All India Trade Test Procedure for the Craftsmen Training Scheme Under the Aegis of NCVT

4.1 INTRODUCTION

1. All India Trade Tests (AITT) are conducted by the National Council for Vocational Training (NCVT) for award of National Trade Certificates (NTCs) to those trainees who qualify the test.
2. The All India Trade Tests are conducted twice in a year in the Month of Jan and July in the Engg & Non Engg Trades under Craftsman Training Scheme.
3. All India Trade Tests are held twice a year in the month of February and August for Multi-Skilling Courses (Broad Based Basic Training and Advanced Training for CoEs and restructured pattern under CTS in MITIs).

4.2 ELIGIBILITY OF THE TRAINEES TO APPEAR IN ALL INDIA TRADE TEST(FOR REGULAR TRAINEES)

The following categories of trainees/candidates are eligible to appear in the All India Trade Test for award of National Trade Certificates:

1. Trainees of Government and Private Industrial Training Institutes (ITIs), completing the prescribed period of training in NCVT affiliated trades.
2. Trainees of NCVT affiliated ITIs imparting Multi Skilling Courses /upgraded as CoEs.

4.3 ELIGIBILITY CONDITIONS FOR APPEARING IN ALL INDIA TRADE TEST (AITT) AS A PRIVATE CANDIDATE UNDER CTS.

1. The applicant should have the minimum prescribed entry qualification for a particular trade under CTS in which he/she is desirous of appearing as private candidate.
2. The applicant should possess a minimum of 3 years' experience in the relevant trade in establishments implementing Apprenticeship Training Scheme/small establishments covered under Factories Act, 1948, or Registered with any government/local authorities.
3. SCVT Certificate holder who has received institutional training in the same trade with the same duration of training period and entry qualification.
4. There should be All India Trade Test by SCVT for all the candidates who are desirous of appearing in the All India Trade Test under the aegis of NCVT as private candidates. All those, who qualify the SCVT test, may be permitted by the State Director to appear in the AITT under NCVT.
5. Private candidates from establishments covered under the Apprentices Act, 1961, and sponsored candidates of ITIs and SCVT certificate holders (above III), may be exempted from appearing in the All India Trade Test to be conducted by the SCVT.
6. Apprentices under the Apprentices Act, 1961 who have failed six times in the All India Trade Tests for the National Apprenticeship Certificate can appear as private candidates in the corresponding trade under CTS only. This will be only applicable to such apprentices who have not qualified earlier for award of National Trade Certificate by the NCVT.
7. Private candidate will have to appear in all the exam of semester for the concerned trades under CTS from the session commencing from August 2013.

DGE&T –1(02)/2013-CD dated 8th Oct. 13
(DGE&T –19(20)/2010-CD, dated 2.11.2010)

4.4. The schedule of All India Trade Test will be announced by Secretary, National Council, for Vocational Training (NCVT) and notified on the DGE&T website and intimated to the State Governments two months in advance.

4.5. 1. Secretary, National Council for Vocational Training makes arrangements to set question papers both for practical as well as theory (related instruction) including the bill of material, if necessary, for each trade and instructions for assessment by appointing suitable experts, as far as possible, from the industry six months in advance of the All India Trade Test.

DGE&T will supply the All India Trade Test question papers to all State Governments/U.T Administrations both in Hindi and English languages. **(DGE&T-19(13)92-CD, dated 1.7.92)**

2. While conducting All India Trade Test, question papers should be so designed that elements of allied areas are suitably covered along with the elements of curriculum of the basic trades in order to enable trainees to acquire the required multi-skills according to present-day requirement.

(DGE&T-19(7)92-CD, dated 19.8.92)

4.6. The question papers will be moderated by Board of Moderators consisting of technical experts of the trade concerned, representatives of the recognized engineering associations with the Secretary, National Council for Vocational Training, as the convener. Some local experts may also be co-opted by the Chair person to assist the Moderation Board if and when their assistance is required. The Moderation Board will finish their proceedings six months in advance of All India Trade Tests due to be held.

4.7. Trainees with minimum 80% attendance are eligible to take the test. But, if a trainee fails to put in 80% minimum attendance for any reasons beyond his/her control, he/she may be allowed to take the test, provided that the essential training is not missed. In cases where the essential training is missed, the trainees should not be permitted to take the test, but may be allowed to continue training along with the subsequent batch to make up the deficiency in attendance. Trainees/who put in 80% attendance but could not appear for the test due to sudden illness or for reasons beyond their control at the time of examinations, can appear for the subsequent test, on the production of a certificate from the Doctor from Government Hospital. For all purposes this may be treated as the trainee's first attempt to appear in the All India Trade Test.

4.8. Examination fee will be charged from the trainees appearing for the test at the following rates:

1. Regular trainees(first attempt) : ₹25/- for both one year and two years course
2. Regular trainees (second and subsequent attempts) : ₹30/- for each attempt
3. Private trainees : ₹50/-

(DGE&T-19(13)/95-CD, dated 30.7.96)

4.9. The following rates of trade-testing expenses per trainee have been prescribed for the Craftsman Training Scheme:

1.	Remuneration to the examiner	...	₹125.00
2.	Cost of Raw Material	...	₹75.00
3.	TA & DA to examiners	...	₹20.00
4.	Remuneration to Invigilators, Chairperson, Superintendents and Group-C and D staff		₹60.00
			₹270.00

4.10 BREAK UP OF REMUNERATION TO THE EXAMINERS

The break-up of the total remuneration is as follows:

1. Practical, including oral : ₹50/- (for all practical relating to the trade per trainee)
2. Trade Theory : ₹25- (for all trade theory papers relating to the trade)
3. Workshop Calculation and Science : ₹25/-(wherever applicable per paper)
4. Engineering Drawing : ₹25/-(wherever applicable per paper)
5. Employability Skills : ₹25/- per trainee

(E-11011/1/2009-TC(Desk), dated 27.2.2009)

4.11 INVIGILATION ALLOWANCES GIVEN TO STAFF ENGAGED FOR TRADE TESTING PURPOSE

Allowances may be paid as per the rates mentioned below:

1. Chairperson, Board of Examiners ... ₹200.00 per day
2. Superintendent of Examination ... ₹150.00 per day
3. Invigilator ... ₹100.00 per day
4. Group 'C' Staff ... ₹100.00 per day
5. Group 'D' staff ... ₹60.00 per day

(E-11011/1/2009-TC (Desk), dated 27.2.2009)

The above rates are applicable for participating in the following All India Trade Tests:

1. Final All India Trade Test under Craftsmen Training Scheme
2. Final All India Trade Test under the Apprenticeship Training Scheme held at ITIs as well as in the establishments other than ITIs
3. All India Skill Competition for Craftsmen as well as Apprentices
4. Skill Competition held at the state level for Craftsmen
5. Skill competitions held at regional level for Apprentices

(DGE&T-12(17)/80-TC, dated 3.3.83)

4.12. The eligible private candidates should apply to the State Director dealing with Craftsmen Training Scheme in the prescribed form, copies of which can be obtained from State Director. The State Director In-charge of Training will verify the authenticity of the particulars of the private candidates keeping in view the guidelines given in Para 5 (I to IV) above before permitting them to the above in the AITT.

4.13. 1. The State Director (Secretary of the State Council) will submit a statement regarding the number of trainees in engineering and non-engineering trades ready to appear for All India Trade Test in the prescribed proforma in triplicate to the Secretary, National Council for Vocational Training, at least three months before the examinations are due to be held. Statements received direct from the Principals of Government and Private ITIs will not be accepted.

2. The State Director of Training should also furnish the names of the State Directorate official dealing with All India Trade Test for Craftsmen Training Scheme along with a separate list of Trade Testing Centres with their full postal addresses email id, mobile phone numbers. and pin code numbers. The total number of candidates appearing for engineering and non-engineering trades against each Trade Testing Centre may also be indicated and supplied to DGE&T.

3. DGE&T will send question papers subject to the submission of the following certificates/undertaking, on the consolidated statements by the State Directors.

"It is to certify that the question papers are indented for the permanently affiliated trades/units in all the following Government and Private ITIs of the State and would be used for the eligible trainees in the trades/units only."

4. The following instructions may be observed while preparing proforma.

   a. Proforma should be printed on a single page and not back to back.
   b. The number of trades and the order of trades should exactly be the same as given in the sample proforma.
   c. Full addresses of Trade Testing Centres need not be given in the consolidated statement. Only the name and place of the centre is sufficient.
   d. The required information may be furnished in one lot and should not be sent in parts or piece-meal.
   e. The serial number once allotted to a particular centre should not be changed in the subsequent pages/statements, i.e. a particular centre should have the same serial number on each page/statement.
   f. The indent in the old proforma would not be accepted.

(DGE&T-18011/1/91-TIC, dated 24.4.91).

4.14. The bill of materials and the special tools, instruments and gauges required to conduct the practical test in each trade will be sent one month in advance of All India Trade Test to the Principal of the institute, where All India Trade Test are to be held, by the *Director of Training*, Secretary, National Council for Vocational Training.

Requisite/raw materials, etc., as per the quantities indicated in the bills of materials and the special tools, instruments and gauges required for All India Trade Test will be kept ready by the Principals concerned at least two weeks before the All India Trade Test.

4.15. Each trainee will be allotted a roll number. The required test pieces, where necessary, will be stamped or punched with corresponding roll number by the Principals concerned before submitting the test piece to the examiner. Before starting the work, each trainee will be given a test piece (except in a trade where this is not possible) bearing the roll number allotted to him/her. No second test piece or components will be supplied by the Board of Examiners, unless it has been proved to their satisfaction that the particular test piece could not be worked on due to some inherent defect in it, or due to circumstances beyond the trainee's control.

4.16. Each trainee will be provided with a badge indicating his/her trade and roll number. These badges should bear the signature of the Principal and should be displayed by the trainees on the left-hand front pocket of the shirt. The trainees who do not have the badges, will not be allowed to enter the examination hall/workshop.

1.17. The concerned Principal will prepare a seating plan allotting seats to candidates and exhibit it in the examination hall in respect of written tests. The seating arrangements should be so arranged that no two trainees of the same trade sit side by side.

4.18. Arrangements to appoint two invigilators for the examination will be made by the Principal concerned. It may, however, be ensured that an Instructor belonging to a particular trade should not be appointed as an invigilator in his/her own trade at his/her own institute and out of two invigilators, one should be a government employee.

4.19. The concerned Principal will arrange to keep ready in advance an adequate number of answer books of sizes 215 mm x 325 mm (8 .1/2" x 13" approx.) with provision of sufficient quantity of spare papers, drawing sheets, etc. To guard against misuse, each answer book should be stamped on the top cover page and the first page inside the book, before they are issued to candidates. The supplementary books should also be similarly stamped. The pages inside the answer books should be serially numbered. Care should be taken to see that no blank answer book is taken out of the examination hall by the candidates.

4.20. The front cover page of the answer book should contain the following information:

(i) Roll Number (ii) Subject (iii) Date (iv) Name of institute

Particulars against each of the above items should be filled in by the candidates. No name should be written anywhere in the answer book or drawing sheets. Besides the above, it should also carry the following instructions to the trainees on the front page:

Instructions for Trainees

a. A 38 mm (1.5) margin should be left on the left-hand side of the answer book.
b. Answers should be written on one side of the page leaving the other for calculation and rough work.
c. Written matter not required to be examined should be scored out with a line across the page.
d. On no account papers from answers sheet should be torn.
e. Trainees found engaged in malpractices may be disqualified from the entire All India Trade Test by the Chairperson.
f. Trainees will not write their names anywhere in the answer books or drawing sheets.

4.21. Requisite number of question papers will be collected by the respective Centre Superintendent from Banks in sealed covers at least one hour before the final examinations are due to commence.

4.22. The sealed covers containing the question papers should be handed over by the Principals to the Chairperson of the Local Board of Examiners who will open them in the presence of other examiners 15 minutes before the commencement of the examination.

4.23. The trainees will take their seats in the examination hall 10 minutes before the commencement of the examination.

4.24. The trainees should not be allowed to bring any book or piece of written or blank paper in the examination hall. The invigilators should warn the trainees in this respect before distributing the examination papers.

4.25. The answer books should be distributed to the trainees just 5 minutes before the commencement of the examination.

4.26. Necessary directions should be given by the invigilators to the trainees for filling up the particulars on the front cover page of the answer book correctly.

4.27. In case a trainee adopts unfair means, he/she will be punished as per the recommendation given in Paragraph 4.54.

4.28. The question papers for practical tests as well as theory papers should not be modified by the Local Board of Examiners. If the materials, as specified in the Bill of Materials, are not available for the practical tests, only dimensions may be slightly modified according to their availability. All the operations/skills included in the practical test must be carried out by the trainees and no modification in this respect should be made by the Local Board of Examiners. If any alteration in the practical test becomes inescapable due to non-availability of certain machines or equipment, this may be done only in exceptional cases. A detailed report regarding such modifications and the reasons thereof should be submitted immediately to the State Director of Training (Secretary, State Council for Vocational Training) who will send a copy of it to the Deputy Director General of Training and Secretary, National Council for Vocational Training.

4.29. At the end of each day of practical examination, the practical jobs and answer sheets, if any should be collected by the examiners and kept as evidence at least for one year. Unfinished jobs, if any, may be issued to the trainees concerned on the next day by the examiners.

4.30. At the end of each theoretical examination, the Principal will arrange to collect the answer books, check them for their correct number and hand them over to the Chairperson of the Local Board of Examiners who, in turn, will hand them over to the respective examiners for evaluations.

4.31.

1. The Board of Examiners will observe the performances of the trainees in the practical examination and evaluate the practical work. Adequate proper attention will be paid to see that the test pieces are the original work of each trainee and bear the corresponding roll number. In case where a marking sheet has been prepared by the paper setters, it must be used for compiling the results, but where a marking sheet has not been provided, the examiners will prepare one. The Chairperson will help the examiners in this connection as well as give the necessary guidance in respect of evaluation of practical jobs, as and when necessary. Detailed marks from these will be entered in the consolidated mark sheets. The Local Board of Examiners will hand over the detailed mark sheets and the consolidated mark sheets together with their comments to the Chairperson, Local Board of Examiners.
2. The Chairperson, Local Board of Examiners, will check the entries in the mark sheets, including the totals. In order to facilitate the placement of trainees, either in employment or in apprenticeship, the Chairperson will declare the results on behalf of the Secretary, State Council for Vocational Training (State Director in-charge of Training), and submit copies of the result sheets in the prescribed Proforma B as appended, to the State Director in-charge of Training (Secretary, State Council).

4.32. The sessional marks should be given by a committee consisting of the Principal and Group Instructor every quarter and such marks should be announced to the trainees concerned from time to time. The trainees who do not obtain the requisite percentage should be warned and their cases kept under close review. Such cases should be brought to the notice of the inspecting officers during their visits.

4.33. In the absence of any member of the Local Board of Examiners, arrangement for conducting the examinations and evaluation will have to be done by the Chairperson with the help of other examiners.

4.34. The respective State Director/Regional Director of Apprenticeship Training may award a maximum of 5 grace marks for engineering trades and 2 grace marks for non-engineering trades (except in the practical).

The grace marks could be awarded in one or more theoretical subjects within the maximum limit of such marks. The State Director may delegate his/her powers for giving grace marks to the Chairperson of the Local Board of Examiners where no centralized evaluation system exists.

For the common subject of Employability Skills, a maximum of 2 grace marks can be awarded to a trainee to make him/her pass the subject.

(DGE&T-12(8)/83-TC, dated 20.8.93)

4.35. Trainees who fail in the test will be discharged along with the others immediately after the All India Trade Test.

4.36. The evaluated answer books for the written papers should be kept under safe custody for one year from the date of the declaration of the trade-test result.

4.37. The trainees in engineering as well as non-engineering trades are entitled to receive the National Trade Certificate immediately after passing the All India Trade Test. Private candidates are also entitled to receive the National Trade Certificate immediately after passing the All India Trade Test. However, provisional certificates will be issued by the Principals to all trainees who qualify in All India Trade Test. Provisional certificates should be issued only in the prescribed form. The Principal may issue mark sheets to the failed trainees on request.

4.38. The National Trade Certificate should be issued only in the prescribed form. If a candidate loses his/her original certificate, a duplicate certificate will be granted on payment of ₹100/-.

4.39. The State Governments and Union Territories will pay remuneration, travelling and daily allowances of examiners, whenever necessary.

4.40 TRADE TESTING CENTRE

1. All India Trade tests may be conducted only in affiliated ITIs having a minimum capacity of 8 units (affiliated to NCVT) and at least 5 years old. However, ITIs affiliated in trades introduced under CTS during the last five-year period and trades which were unique in districts are exempted from the above clause and could be made Trade Testing Centres as per alternatives available passed on State Government permission.

   Also, in exceptional circumstances, the State Director may locate a Trade Testing Centre in an institute having less than 8 units, provided it has all other requisite infrastructural facilities. It would also be ensured that supervision of one government employee, other than the staff members of the institute, is provided at such a centre at the time of All India Trade Test.

   (DGE&T-19(28)/2010-CD, dated 30.8.2010)
2. For ITIs having less than 8 units, practical All India Trade Tests may be conducted in an affiliated ITI having a minimum capacity of 8 units and relevant trade(s) and which is located preferably within a distance of 50 km.
3. For ITIs having less than 8 units of capacity, the theoretical test may be conducted after grouping different small ITIs in a suitable building, if so required.
4. The State Directors, In-charge of Craftsmen Training should ensure that the Trade Testing Centres located by them have all the requisite facilities in terms of tools, equipment and machinery for conducting the practical tests. They should also depute a responsible officer to visit these centres prior to commencement of All India Trade Test to ensure that the required numbers of machines/equipment are in order at these centres. The institutes where the required number of machines/

equipment/tools are not available or are not in a working condition should not be selected as Trade Testing Centres.

4.41 EXAMINERS (FOR PRACTICAL AND THEORY)

1. As far as possible, the evaluation of theoretical subjects should be done centrally by each State Directorate.
2. Answer books of the trainees for each centre should be coded for identification.
3. The practical test should be evaluated at the respective Trade Testing Centre by the examiners and the evaluated practical jobs may be preserved for a minimum period of one year after the declaration of the result. Wherever feasible, the practical test may also be conducted on a centralized basis at the regional level.
4. Examiners called for evaluation should have minimum technical qualification of a diploma in the respective engineering field/discipline. Where diploma holders are not available, the qualifications of the examiners may be suitably relaxed.
5. Examiners may be appointed preferably from polytechnics/engineering colleges/industry of repute, government departments, corporations or from amongst retired qualified personnel possessing requisite qualifications and sufficient experience in the trade/discipline.
6. Each State Directorate shall prepare a panel of examiners according to the above norms and submit the same to Directorate General of Employment and Training for reference. The list submitted must contain the technical qualifications and experience of the proposed examiners.
7. The State Directorate would appoint examiners only from the panel prepared and submitted by them.
8. The State Directorate may also appoint a Chief Examiner for the moderation of examinations.

4.42 SUPERVISORS AND INVIGILATORS

1. The principal of an ITI where tests can be conducted may be appointed as Chairperson/Secretary of the Local Board of Examination in the centre.
2. The Chairperson of the Local Board of Examination may appoint a Superintendent and Supervisor with the approval of the State Director.
3. The State Director/Principal would appoint invigilators for each centre. Invigilators appointed for the test should, as far as possible, not be from the same institute.
4. The State Director would constitute a Flying Squad consisting of senior officers to visit the Trade Testing Centres for surprise check and submit the report to the State Director with a copy endorsed to the Directorate General of Employment & Training, highlighting the various observations made during the visit. The report should be submitted within one week by email from the last date of the trade test.
5. The Directorate General of Employment & Training would also appoint Central Observers, covering at least one centre of each state during the test. The observer would submit a report to the Directorate General of Employment & Training within one week from the last date of the trade test. In case some major deviations from the prescribed norms in conducting All India Trade Test in a centre are brought to the notice of authorities that centre can be debarred for conducting the test for a minimum period of three years and the concerned All India Trade Test can be cancelled by the Secretary, National Council for Vocational Training. Trainees would be asked to re-appear in the subsequent test under the scheme.

4.43 ISSUE OF PRINTED CERTIFICATES

1. The State Director would submit to the Directorate General of Employment & Training the number of trainees appeared and passed trade wise and, institute wise in the Prescribed performa. The details may also be sent in Compact Disk to DGE&T for verification purpose. If data of state is verified, DGE&T will print the certificate in the name of students and forward it to respective state Directorates having Printed signature of secretary NCVT. The secretary, SCVT would counter The certificate in ink before distribution to respective Principal/Regional office. The Principal of concern ITI would also sign on the back before issue to the trainee. For each All India Trade Test conducted in the State/UT within one month of declaration of the result.

(DGE&T-19(23)/2010-CD)

2. Blank certificates duly serial-numbered without facsimile signature of Secretary, National Council for Vocational Training, would be supplied by DGE&T after scrutiny of the test result forwarded by the State Directorate mentioned at S.No. (1) above. The State Directorate after filling the entries and signing the certificates in ink would send these certificates back to the DGE&T Headquarters for obtaining the facsimile signature of Deputy Director General of Training/Secretary, NCVT. The State Director would ensure that these certificates are used for the successful trainees of the All India Trade Test under reference.

4.44 REMUNERATION TO PAPER SETTERS AND MODERATORS FOR THE VARIOUS ALL INDIA TRADE TESTS UNDER THE CRAFTSMEN TRAINING SCHEME AND APPRENTICESHIP TRAINING SCHEME

The following rates or remuneration are payable to the paper setters and moderators in respect of All India Trade Tests conducted under the Craftsmen Training Scheme & Apprenticeship Training Scheme w.e.f 1.4.2007.

1. Craftsmen Training Scheme — ₹400/- per paper
2. All India Skill Competition for Craftsmen — ₹500/- per paper
3. Crafts Instructors Training Scheme — ₹400/- per paper
4. Vocational Training of Women Occupation — ₹400/- per paper
5. Apprenticeship Training Scheme — ₹400/- per paper
6. Regional Competition of Apprentices — ₹500/- per paper
7. All India Skill Competition of Apprentices — ₹500/- per paper
8. Moderation of all types of question papers — ₹100/- per paper

(DGE&T-12(4)/2007-TC, dated 23.3.2007)

4.45 ALL INDIA TRADE TEST IN THE ENGINEERING TRADES

All India Trade Test is conducted by the National Council for Vocational Training in the following five subjects.

1. Practical including sessional work
2. Trade Theory including sessional work
3. Workshop Calculation and Science including sessional work
4. Engineering Drawing including sessional work
5. Employability Skills

S. No.	Subject for All India Trade Test	Maximum Marks for Each Subject	Minimum % Required for Pass	Minimum Marks Required for Pass
1.	Practical (including sessional work)	400 (Practical test:300) (Sessional work:100)	60 %	240
2.	Trade Theory (including sessional work)	120 (Written test paper:100) (Sessional work:20)	40%	48
3.	Workshop Calculation and Science (including sessional work)	60 (Written test paper:50) (Sessional work:10)	40%	24
4.	Engineering Drawing (including sessional work)	70 (Drawing test paper:50) (Sessional work:20)	40%	28
5.	Employability Skills*	50	40%	20
	Total	**700**		**360**

(DGE&T-12(16)/82-TC, dated 24.11.82)

Notes

1. (a) To pass , a trainee has to secure 40% marks exclusively in a trade theory subject and also 40% on the total marks, i.e. the aggregate of theory subject and sessional.

   (b) A trainee, should secure 60% marks in aggregate in practical test and sessional.

(DGE&T-19(15)/92-CD, dated 2.7.92)

2. If a trainee fails in one or more subjects he/she may be permitted to re-appear in the subsequent test.
3. It need not be necessary for a trainee to appear in all the subjects in the first attempt for securing exemption.

(DGE&T-19(15)/91-CD, dated 2.1.92)

The condition for securing 10% more marks on the total of the subject than minimum pass marks in any subject in All India Trade Test under CTS/ATS/CITS is waived off.

(DGE&T-19(9)/95-CD, dated 26.6.96)

4. (a) Five additional chances may be given to a failed trainee within a period of three years to pass the Final All India Trade Test for the award of National Trade Certificate.

(No.DGE&T-12(15)/82-TC, dated 8.1.82)

   (b) For trainees who are not able to avail the additional five chances within the prescribed period of three years because of either the results not being declared on time or due to other unavoidable circumstances such as curfew or natural calamity, etc., the period of three years may be extended suitably to cover the period lost on the merit of the case.

(DGE&T-19(10)95-CD, dated 23.7.1996)

5. Each trainee will submit his/her sessional work to the Chairperson indicating his/her roll number. The Chairperson will give the sessional work to the examiner concerned for evaluation. The evaluation should be done on the basis of the progress cards of the trainee, exercises done by him/her during his/her training period, class notebooks, and records, etc. kept by him/her. The periodical assessment made as mentioned in S.No. 30 above should be kept in view. A few questions related to the trade may be asked by the examiner concerned during the practical test. A few simple questions on employability skills may also be asked.

4.46. In the case of private candidates, there being no sessional work, the total marks and the minimum marks required for a pass for the different subjects will be as follows:

S. No.	Subject for All India Trade Test	Maximum marks for each subject	Minimum % Required for Pass	Minimum Marks Required for Pass pass in each subject
1.	Practical	300	60%	180
2.	Trade Theory	100	40%	40
3.	Workshop Calculation and Science	50	40%	20
4.	Engineering Drawing	50	40%	20
5.	*Employability Skills	50	40%	20
	Total	**550**		**280**

(DGE&T–12(16)/82-TC, dated 24.11.82)

4.47 ALL INDIA TRADE TESTS IN THE NON-ENGINEERING TRADES

The maximum and minimum marks required to pass different subjects will be as follows.

S. No.	Subject for All India Trade Test	Maximum Marks	Minimum % Required for Pass	Minimum Marks Required for Pass
1.	Practical (including sessional work)	120 (Practical test:100) (Sessional work:20)	60%	72
2.	Trade Theory	30	40%	12
3.	*Employability Skills	50	40%	20
	Total	**200**		**104**

Notes:

1. In case of private candidates, there being no sessional work, the maximum marks will be 180 and other conditions will remain the same.
2. The State Government will issue the above instructions to all the officers concerned for conducting and evaluating the All India Trade Test conducted under the aegis of NCVT & for issue of certificates etc.

***(DGE&T 19(17)/2010-CD date 12 April 2012)**

4.48 ALL INDIA TRADE TEST PROCEDURE FOR MULTI SKILL TRADES

Guidelines for Trainees to pass the Theory papers.

1. In all, two theory papers would be conducted. Three modules as indicated in the marking scheme, would be covered in each paper. The question paper would have three parts covering questions of individual modules separately.
2. For theory papers, Institutes are advised to supply one separate answer sheet for each part duly earmarked, i.e. three separate answer sheets per trainee would be required for each paper. This would facilitate the evaluation of these answer sheets by the concerned trade experts.

3. Trainees should be intimated well in advance that they have to write answers for each module in the prescribed answer sheets. No marks would be given in case the answers are given in wrong sheets.
4. Trainees are required to secure a minimum of 40% marks excluding Sessional Work in each theory paper and a minimum of 20% marks in each module for a pass.

4.49 GUIDELINES FOR TRAINEES TO PASS THE PRACTICAL PAPERS

1. There will be two practicals, each of 200 marks, having six to eight hours duration each. The practical will continue for two days. Practical I comprises of the skill as per syllabi Modules 01,02,03 and Practical II comprises of Skill Modules 04,05,06
2. Both practical papers would be opened on the first day of practical on the scheduled date.
3. For practical test, trainees are required to secure a minimum of 60% marks in practical including sessional.

4.50 GENERIC MODULE

1. Workshop calculation science & Engineering Drawing (WCS&ED)
   The question paper will have two separate parts, one each for Module 7 and 8 as indicated in the marking scheme. Institutes are advised to supply one separate answer sheet for each module.
   Workshop Calculation and Science and Engineering Drawing Question Papers (Module 07 & 08)
   (i) The question paper will have two parts A and B, each for Module 07 and Module 08, each of 50 marks and 2 hours duration each
   (ii) Trainees are required to secure a minimum of 40% marks in aggregate to pass the WCS&ED Module and minimum of 20% marks in a module.
2. Entrepreneurship and Communication Skill
   There would be one question paper. Trainees are required to secure a minimum of 33% marks to pass the paper. The question paper for this subject shall be of 2 hours duration having 50 marks.
3. Employability Skills
   From the session starting from August 2013, the subject Entrepreneurship & Communal Skills will be replace by Employability Skills.

(DGE&T 19 (17)/2010-CD date 19th Mar 2013)

The same marking scheme of Employments skills for CTS course will be applicable.

Evaluation Evaluation of the answer books and practical exercises shall be carried out as per the existing system in vogue in other schemes under NCVT.

Marking Scheme for Broad Based Basic Training for Production and Manufacturing Electrical, Electronics, Automobile, IT Sector, Plastic Processing, Refrigeration and Air Conditionings, Instrumentation, Chemical, Fabrication, Agriculture Machinery, Process Plant Maintenance and Hospitality implemented at Centres of Excellence

S. No.	No. of Test	Skill Area, both for Practical and Theory as per Modules	Marks Allotted	Duration	Passing Marks
1.	Practical I	Modules 01, 02, 03	200	6–8 hours }	60%
2.	Practical II	Modules 04, 05, 06 Sessional Work (Practical)	200 100	6–8 hours } 500 }	60%

3.	Theory I	Modules 01, 02, 03	100	3 hours }	40%
4.	Theory II	Modules 04, 05, 06 Sessional Work (Theory)	100 20	3 hours } 220 }	40%
5.	Workshop Calculation and Science, and Engineering Drawing	* Modules 07, 08 Sessional Work	100 20	4 hours } } 120 }	40%
6.	Employability skills	Sessional Work	50 10	2 hours } } 60 }	40%
		Total	900		

* For "Hospitality Sector," Module 07 and 08 are Hotel Accountancy and Hygiene in place of Workshop Calculation and Science and Engineering Drawing

Marking Scheme for Broad Based Basic Training for Leather Goods & Footwear, Apparel implemented at Centres of Excellence

S. No.	No. of Test	Skill Area, both for Practical and Theory as per Modules	Marks Allotted	Duration	Passing Marks
1.	Practical I	Modules 01, 02, 03	200	6–8 hours }	60%
2.	Practical II	Modules 04, 05, 06 Sessional Work (Practical)	200 100	6–8 hours } 500 }	60%
3.	Theory I	Modules 01, 02, 03	100	3 hours }	40%
4.	Theory II	Modules 04, 05, 06 Sessional Work (Theory)	100 20	3 hours } 220 }	40%
5.	Employability skills	Sessional Work	50 10	2 hours } } 60 }	40%
		Total	780		

Marking Scheme for Broad Based Basic Training for Construction and Wood Working, Food Processing implemented at Centres of Excellence

S. No.	No. of Test	Skill Area, both for Practical and Theory as per Modules	Marks Allotted	Duration	Passing Marks
1.	Practical I	Modules 01, 02, 03	200	6–8 hours }	60%
2.	Practical II	Modules 04, 05, 06 Sessional Work (Practical)	200 100	6–8 hours } 500 }	60%
3.	Theory I	Modules 01, 02, 03	100	3 hours }	40%
4.	Theory II	Modules 04, 05, 06 Sessional Work (Theory)	100 20	3 hours } 220 }	40%

5.	Workshop Calculation and Science, and Basic Computer Application	* Modules 07, 08 Sessional Work	100 20	4 hours } } 120 }	40%
6.**	Employability Skills	Sessional Work	50 10	2 hours } } 60 }	40%
		Total	900		

Note: * For the sector **"Food Processing,"** as Workshop Calculation and Science is not covered in course curricula therefore, All India Trade Test will be only for Basic Computer Application for 120 marks including sessional. **The subject Entrepreneurship and Communication Skill has been replaced by Employability Skills.

REMARKS:

- Marking scheme for different sectors would be applicable to all the trainees under the scheme.
- No grace marks in any subject would be allotted to the trainees under the scheme.
- The trainees after appearing in BBBT may be provisionally allowed to take admission in Advanced Module without waiting for the result. The failed trainees would be allowed to appear for All India Trade Test of BBBT (failed subject) and Advance Module in the subsequent All India Trade Test. The result of advanced module would be declared only after qualifying the failed subject of BBBT.
- For all other issues, guidelines and instructions relating to Trade Testing Procedure for conducting the All India All India Trade Test under the Craftsmen Training Scheme would be applicable to the trainees undergoing training at Centres of Excellence.

Marking scheme for Advanced modules of Multi skill Courses offered at upgraded Government and Private ITIs under CTS

S. No.	Subject for Trade Test	Maximum Marks	Minimum % Required for Pass	Minumum Marks required for Passing (each subject)
1	Practical test Practical sessional	300 + 100 = 400	60% in practical and aggregate	240
2	Theory (written test) Theory (sessional work)	100 + 20 = 120	40% in theory test and aggregate	48

(DGE&T-19(15)/2010-CD)

4.51 CERTIFICATION

National Trade Certificate

For Conventional Craftsmen Training Scheme The final All-India Trade Tests are conducted by the National Council for Vocational Training after completion of the prescribed period of training and successful trainees are awarded the National Trade Certificates in the trades concerned **(Appendix IIIA)**. The National Trade Certificates are recognised for recruitment to the subordinate posts and services under the Government of India for which a Certificate in Craftsmanship/NTC is prescribed as the requisite qualification.

Recognition of Dipolomas/Certificates Awarded under Craftsmen/Displaced Persons Training Schemes The Government of India has decided to recognise for purpose of recruitment to subordinate posts and services under the Central Government, the diploma in Craftsmanship awarded to trainees admitted under the craftsmen/displaced persons training schemes before February, 1959 **(Appendix VIIA)** and the National Trade Certificates awarded thereafter in the trades mentioned in **(Appendix VII)**. The Diploma in Craftsmenship awarded by the Directorate General of Resettlement and Employment (now Directorate General of Employment and Training) will be deemed to be equal to the National Trade Certificate awarded under the aegis of National Council for Vocational Training.

It has been decided to recognise the certificates awarded by the All India Handicrafts Broad, New Delhi in the trades of (i) toy making, (ii) mat making, (iii) doll making, (iv) Clay work and pottery wares, and (v) wood carving, for purpose of recruitment to the subordinate posts and services under the Central Government as these course are run at the craftsmen level.

The Government of India have decided to recognise for the purpose of recruitment to subordinate posts and services under the Central Government, proficiency certificate awarded to successful trainees under the vocational training scheme (now defunct) for disabled ex-serviceman of the DGR & E (Now DGE&T) for the trade of Coir Weaving (18 months course.)

The central government have decided that the recognition previously given to Diplomas in Craftsmanship in the trades of Draughtsman (Civil) and Draughtsman (Mechanical) awarded by the DGT&E be extended to the National Trade Certificate in Draughtsman ship awarded by the National Council for Vocational Training to those candidates who have studied or been trained at recognized institutes or centres affiliated to the National Council.

The Government of India have decided to recognise for the purpose of recruitment to subordinate posts and service under the Central Government the "Diploma in Craftsmanship" awarded to successful trainees under the Craftsmen/Disabled Persons Training Schemes of the Directorate General of Resettlement and Employment (now Directorate General of Employment and Training) before February, 1959, in the trade of Mechanic (General).

Procedure for the recognition of trade certificates in the trades other than those included in the DGE&T training schemes awarded by different Ministries/Departments of the Government of India is contained in (**Appendix XXIV**).

The Government of India decided to recognise the certificates awarded by the Heavy Vehicles Mechanic-cum-Drivers Training Centre at Mana in the trade of Heavy Vehicles Mechanics-cum-Drivers for the purpose of recruitment to the subordinate posts and services under the Central Government.

All trainees admitted in the Training Centre for Adult Deaf (TCAD) Hyderabad (Andhra Pradesh) from the Session starting from 1st August 1997 will be required to appear in all the subject of the trade in All India Trade Test conducted under the aegis of NCVT for Craftsmen Training Scheme and will get National Trade Certificate after passing the Trade Test as per existing Rules.

(No. DGET-19/26/96-CD, Dt.21.5.1997)

For Multiskill Training and Craftsmen Training

National Trade Certificates of one-year Broad Based Basic Training as well as for Advanced Modules are awarded to the successful trainees as per the format of certificate given at (**Appendix IIIC & IIID**).

Specialized modular courses are organized during the last phase of training to bridge the skill gaps keeping in view the needs of industry in the region. The testing and certification for the last phase is done jointly by State Government and Industry **(Appendix IIIE)**. These certificates are recognized by the NCVT. Detailed guidelines and certificates are at (**Appendix IV**).

(DGE&T-19(1)/2006-CD, dated 22.10. 2007

4.52 RECOGNITION OF CERTIFICATES OF BBBT & ADVANCED MODULE

Recognition of NTC

The Government of India, on the recommendation of the National Council for Vocational Training, has recognized National Trade Certificate (NTC) of one-year BBBT as well as the NTC for Advanced Modules awarded to successful trainees for the purpose of recruitment to subordinate posts and services under the Central Government

(DGE&T-19(1)/2006-CD, dated 22.10.2007)

4.53 RECOMMENDED PUNISHMENT FOR USING UNFAIR MEANS IN ALL INDIA TRADE TEST CONDUCTED UNDER THE AEGIS OF NCVT

S. No.	Nature of Offence/Unfair Means	Recommended Punishment
1.	Writing his/her name or any distinctive remark on the answer book	The Chairperson of the examination may disqualify the trainee from passing the examination in that year. For any further punishment, a committee consisting of the Head of the institute and two senior staff members, preferably of Grade-A or B, should conduct an enquiry and recommend the amount of punishment including debarring from appearing in subsequent examinations up to a period of 3 years. However, the trainee may be given an opportunity to explain his/her conduct before the final decision of awarding the punishment is taken by the concerned authorities. The State Director or Director of Institute under DGE&T will have full authority to give a final decision in the matter.
2.	Writing answers on the question paper	
3.	Leaving the examination hall without permission of the invigilation staff until the paper is finished	
4.	Disorderly conduct/rude behaviour/impersonation/threatening the invigilation staff	
5.	Found in possession of indiscriminate material on his/her person	
6.	Exchanging answer book with other trainee	
7.	Found copying in the examination or giving/receiving assistance of any kind or attempting to do so	
8.	Tearing off any page of the answer book/supplementary answer book/smuggling out the answer book	
9.	Contacting or trying to contact any other person during examination time	
10.	While checking answer book, it is noticed that the trainee has copied from some book or from the answer book of another trainee	
11.	Using or attempting to use any other undesirable method or means in connection with the examinations	

4.54 STRICT MEASURES TO ENSURE CONDUCT OF ALL INDIA TRADE TEST AS PER NCVT NORMS

The lapses on the part of the administration in the Trade Testing Centres call for strict measures as otherwise the All India Trade Tests being conducted on behalf of NCVT would be reduced to a mockery. Therefore, the centres in which such lapses are noticed should be debarred from holding the subsequent tests for a minimum period of two years and in certain exceptional cases, the concerned institutes/trade could also be de-affiliated and de-recognized by the NCVT.

Further, in order to have proper supervision of the All India Trade Test, the State Government/UT administration should constitute Flying Squads by deputing senior officers to cover a few selected centres under their respective jurisdiction. The concerned officers should check and ensure implementation of trade testing norms prescribed by NCVT.

(DGE&T-2((6)/86-CD, dated 17.2.86)

The result of the All India Trade Tests under Craftsmen Training Scheme (CTS) and Apprenticeship Training Scheme (ATS) should be declared within two months of the date of the last All India Trade Test.

(DGE&T-19(14)/96-CD, dated 14.5.97)

4.55 RE-EVALUATION OF ANSWER BOOKS OF ALL INDIA TRADE TEST

1. Re-evaluation of answer book is not permissible
2. In case of failed candidates, the answer book would only be checked to the extent of re-totaling the marks and checking the portion left unmarked, if any.
3. For this purpose, a fee of ₹10/- would be charged per paper from the failed candidates only.
4. For other trainees, a fee of ₹25/- would be charged for carrying out (2) above.
5. The time limit for application for such re-valuation would be one month from the date of declaration of results.

4.56 ISSUE OF DUPLICATE TRADE CERTIFICATES

1. The trainees should apply for the issue of duplicate certificates to the Principals of training institutes where they had undergone training. The Principals should ensure that the trainees have deposited a sum of ₹100 *, the prescribed fee for the issue of duplicate certificate, in a treasury and the receipt of treasury to this effect is produced. The Principal thereupon should put up an indent for such certificate mentioning the correct type of certificates for which he/she is entitled, i.e. the National Trade Certificate (indented for regular trainees) or the National Trade Certificates (indented for Private Candidates) or the DGE&T Craftsmen Diploma, to the State Director of Training. The State Director of Training will then supply the blank forms to the Principals to get the entries filled up neatly and correctly by a good hand preferably by a draughtsman and thereafter forward the same to the State Director (Secretary, State Council) with the information as under:
   (i) Name of the trainee
   (ii) Institute where he/she had his training
   (iii) The period of training from ____ to ____
   (iv) The year in which he/she passed
   (v) The trade in which he/she appeared and passed.

   In addition, a certificate to the effect that the trainee has deposited the fee of ₹100 in a Treasury and the treasury receipt has been produced should be forwarded. The State Director will then, after signing the certificates, forward them to the Secretary, National Council for Vocational Training (Director of Training, DGE&T), together with the above information and certificates.

These certificates, after the counter-signature, will be returned to the State Directors who will pass them on to the Principals concerned for issuing them to the trainees. The word Duplicate should be stamped at the top of the front side of the certificate.
* Revised through DGE&T communication

(DGE&T-(DGE&T-9(09)/2003-TC, dated 14.7. 2004)

2. The names of trades should be correctly mentioned in the certificates

4.57 ALL INDIA SKILLS COMPETITION UNDER CRAFTSMEN TRAINING SCHEME

In order to foster a spirit of healthy competition among the trainees of the institutes and with a view to raise the standard of their skills, the scheme of holding an All India Skills Competition was started in 1964.

Trades covered in this competition are **Turner, Fitter, Machinist, Electrician, Welder (G&E), Mechanic (Motor Vehicle), Electronic Mechanic, Draughtsman (Mechanical), Instrument Mechanic, Mechanic Machine Tool Maintenance, Tool and Die Maker (Dies &Moulds), Tool and Die Maker (Press Tools, Jigs and Fixtures), Refrigeration and Air Conditioning Mechanic, Mechanic (Diesel) and Wireman.**

Only the trainees under the regular Craftsmen Training Scheme are eligible to compete in the All India Skills Competition.

(DGE&T-19(6)/89-CD, dated 31.3.89)

1. Levels of Competition

The All India Skills Competition is conducted in two levels—State level and All India level.

(i) State-Level Competition The best trainees in each of the 15 trades from each ITI are eligible to participate in this competition. Based on this competition, the best trainees amongst the qualified trainees in each of the 15 trades are selected at the state level. MITI trainees from various places are allowed to compete with the ITI trainees of respective states as per the prescribed procedure to make them eligible for competing at the All India Skills Competition.

(DGE&T-19 (10)/90-CD, dated 21.5.90)

(ii) All India Level Competition The best trainees in each of the eligible 15 trades at the state-level competition are eligible to compete in the All India competition. The best trainees amongst the qualified trainees in each of the 15 trades are selected based on this competition at the All India level.

2. Subjects for the Competition and Allocation of Marks

The marking scheme, with the subjects for the competition, is given below:

Sl. No	Subject	Maximum Marks	Minimum Qualifying Marks
1.	Trade Practical	300	180
2.	Trade Theory	100	50
3.	Workshop Calculation and Science	50	25
4.	Engineering Drawing	50	25
	Total	**500**	**280**

The competitors who fail even in one subject are declared 'Not Qualified'. From amongst the qualified competitors, only the best are declared in each trade, that is those who score the highest total marks and not less than 70% marks in practical.

3. Eligibility Norms for All India Skill Competition

(i) Candidates passing with grace marks are not considered eligible at any level under the All India Skill Competition.

(ii) If more than one candidate scores the same highest aggregate marks in the All India Trade Test or All India Skill Competitions, the candidate who scores more marks in the Trade Practical will be declared eligible.

(iii) If aggregate and marks in Trade Practical are same for more than one candidate then all such candidates will be declared eligible.

(iv) As the subject of Social Studies Emp Skill has no direct bearing on the skill competitiveness of trainees, the marks obtained in this subject are not counted for selecting trainees to appear in skill competitions held under CTS/ATS.

(DGE&T-19(9)/93-CD, dated 21 .9.93)

(v) Under CTS, when an MTI/MITI trainee stands first in a particular trade at the state-level competition, the trainee who stands second in the trade and belongs to the state will be permitted to appear in the All India Skill Competitions.

(DGE&T-19(13)/96-CD, dated 19.5.1997)

(vi) When a state does not conduct State Skills Competition, an MTI/MITI trainee who stands first in the All India Trade Test for craftsmen will be permitted to participate in the All India Skill Competitions.

(DGE&T-19(13)96-CD, dated 19.5.1997)

4. Declaration of the Best Trainee at all India Level Competition

The competitor, who stands first, after qualifying in the competition, will be declared the best trainee (winner) in his/her trade, provided he/she scores a minimum of 70% of the maximum marks in the practical test.

5. Awards Under the Scheme

The following awards shall be given under the scheme:

(i) Merit Certificate to the best trainee in each of the 15 trades in each Industrial Training Institute **(Appendix XXI)**

(ii) Merit Certificate to the best trainee in each trade at the state-level competition.

(iii) Merit Certificate and cash prize of ₹50,000 to the best trainee of each trade

(DGE&T-19(25)/2010-CD, dated 15.10.2010)

(iv) Merit Certificate to the best ITI in each trade whose trainee stands first in the All India Level Competition in the respective trade as per proforma furnished given at **(Appendix XXII)**.

(v) Running shield to the state whose trainees secure highest total marks in all the trades in the All India Level Competition.

(vi) The Silver Trophy is allowed to be retained by the winning state who wins the Best State Award during All India Skill Competitions for Craftsmen consecutively for three years. This provision is being followed from 34th All India Skill Competitions for Craftsmen held in December 1997 onwards (Merit Certificate Proforma given at **(Appendix XXIII)**).

6. Travelling Allowance/Daily Allowance

The following allowances are given for the competitors under the scheme:

(i) Travelling Allowance Reimbursement of the travelling expenditure would be limited to second-class train fare for the shortest distance between the hometown/place of duty/place of training to the place of All India Skill Competitions/place of function for awards and back. Shortest distance is calculated between railway stations nearest to both the places under consideration.

(ii) Daily Allowance DA as applicable to a 'Group-C' Central/State government employee at the minimum of scale as per rules for the complete period of competition shall be paid. Journey period shall be taken into account for the payment of DA.

(DGE&T-8(3)/85-TC, dated 3.10.85)

7. Incentives Offered to the Instructional Staff of ITIs Under The Scheme

(i) A cash award of ₹3000 and a Merit Certificate to the concerned ITI instructor of the trade, whose trainee is adjudged the best trainee in the skill competition at the state level

(ii) A cash award of ₹1500 and a Merit Certificate to each ITI instructor (Allied Trade, Workshop Calculation and Science and Engineering Drawing) whose trainee is adjudged the best trainee in the skill competition at the state level

(iii) A cash award of ₹6000 to the concerned ITI instructor of the trade whose trainee is adjudged the best trainee in the skill competition at the All India level

(iv) A cash award of ₹3000 to each ITI instructor (Allied Trade, Workshop Calculation and Science and Engineering Drawing) whose trainee is adjudged the best trainee in the skill competition of all India level.

(DGE&T-19(25)/2010-CD, dated 15-10-2010)

8. Other Awards in Trades Not Covered Under all India Skill Competitions

It is purely optional for State Governments to provide

(i) A cash award of ₹2000 and a Merit Certificate to every trainee who stands first in the trade at the state level, excluding the 15 trainees already covered in the All India Skill Competition

(ii) A cash award of ₹1500 to each Trade Instructor, Allied Trade Instructor, Workshop Science and Calculation and Engineering Drawing Instructors whose trainees stood first at the state level

The implementation of the proposal is, however, left to the discretion of the State Governments.

(DGE&T-19(9)/92-CD, dated June '92)

Appendices

Appendix I

"Article of Memorandum of Association"

For registering the State Council of Vocation & Training (SCVT) as Society under the Societies Registration Act, 1860

(Draft Model)

1. NAME OF THE SOCIETY

The name of the Society shall be "State Council of Vocational Training Society of ------------ State."

2. REGISTERED OFFICE OF THE SOCIETY

The Registered Office of the Society shall be situated at ____________.(full Address)

3. AIMS AND OBJECTIVES

Aims of the Society

(i) To assist in improvement of standard of vocational training and skill development with a view to develop competent manpower catering to the need of various industries and other organizations within the state.

(ii) To develop and strengthen vocational training at all levels through formal and non-formal mode, with need based courses of adequate quality level, curriculum, learning resources and teaching-learning process, assessment and certification

(iii) To initiate steps to increase awareness amongst the unskilled youth about learning skills through proper campaigns and to motivate them to acquire various skills which can earn them employment

(iv) To ensure effective implementation of various schemes of skill development, both by the NCVT as well as their own need based courses

(v) To encourage Private–Public Partnership in the establishment of new world class vocational training in the emerging areas of technology and also to strengthen Industry–ITI interaction for enhancing employability of unemployed youth

(vi) To develop a proper feedback mechanism to bridge the gap (if any) between the demand/supply of training needs and requirements in their area

Main Objects to be Pursued by the Society

(i) To assess emerging skill requirements in the region and suggest changes in the training courses being run in the state

(ii) To obtain short-term, medium-term and long-term requirement of skilled workforce and take steps to produce graduates in the ITI accordingly

(iii) To review training needs of instructors and administrative/office staff of the ITI and arrange for their training programmes

(iv) To assess the requirement of funds for the ITI and make recommendations to the State Government on the funds provided by it to the ITI out of its Annual Budget

(v) To ensure implementation of instructions/guidelines contained in the Training Manual for Craftsmen Training

(vi) To plan and execute Skill Development Programmes to prepare youth for self-employment and for various jobs available in industrial and service sectors

(vii) To develop competency-based curricula, and to train and certify school drop-outs, labourers working in unorganised sectors and service sectors, and unskilled workers engaged in various industries

(viii) To prepare need based training programmes of different levels as per the requirement of various groups of industrial sectors, which are recognized at national and international levels and also to recognize such programmes for further education

(ix) To develop suitable feedback mechanism to understand the training needs, requirement and shortfalls in the area of operation of the Society, through their field offices and institutes, and to act upon them

(x) To plan suitable campaigns/advertisements to increase awareness amongst the youth about the positive aspects of learning and acquiring various skills and related employment opportunities

(xi) To develop a flexible delivery mechanism to impart training in part time, weekends, full time, onsite/offsite mode keeping view of the following:

  (a) To plan and monitor National Skill Development Policy at State level.

  (b) To frame policy and programmes to link non-formal vocational training with the formal education system and to develop a system of recognizing prior acquired learning

  (c) To converge and develop available training resources in the state through Public–Private Partnership

  (d) To provide access to vocational education and training with inclusive growth for all the groups of the Society

  (e) To provide training of trainers, to promote innovation in training and also to render consultancy services

  (f) To award certificates, diplomas and other distinctions to trained manpower and set norms for quality and standards of the vocational training system

(g) To affiliate institutes as vocational training providers on payment of prescribed fee

(h) To forecast the needs of skilled manpower to cater to the needs of various stakeholders in the state on a regular basis

(i) To institute and award scholarships, prizes and medals in accordance with the rules and bye laws to the meritorious trainees

(j) To fix and demand such fees and other charges as may be laid down in the bye laws made under the rules of the Society

(k) To establish, maintain and manage the land, building, other infrastructure and assets of the Society for institutional purposes

(l) To create, with the prior approval of the State Government, administrative, technical, ministerial and other posts under the Society and to make appointments thereto

(m) To interact and co-operate with any educational institute, training organization and industrial organization having objects wholly or partly similar to those of the Society

(n) To develop continuing education programmes for the personnel in the organized and unorganized sectors in the state

(o) To make rules and regulations and bye-laws for the conduct of the affairs of the Society and to add, to amend, to vary or rescind them from time to time with the approval of the State Government

(p) To establish a network with similar organization for exchange of expertise, information/documents and publications

(q) To acquire and hold property, provided that the prior approval of the State Government is obtained for the acquisition of immovable property

(r) To deal with any such property belonging to or vested in the Society in such manner as the Society may deem fit for advancing its objects, in the best interest of the Society, provided that prior approval of the State Government is obtained for this purpose

4. INCOME AND PROPERTY OF THE SOCIETY

(i) The income and property of the Society, howsoever derived, shall be applied towards the promotion of the aims and objects thereof as set forth in this Memorandum of Association.

(ii) No portion of the income and property of the Society shall be paid or transferred as dividends, bonus or by way of profits or otherwise, to any persons who at any time are or have been members of the Society or to any one claiming through them, provided that nothing herein contained shall prevent the payment in good faith of honoraria, perquisites, facilities of any nature to the officers and employees as the Governing Council thinks fit in return of any services rendered to the Society.

Funds of the Society

(i) The society shall maintain a fund to which shall be credited

  (a) All money provided by the Central and State Government;

  (b) All fees and other charges received by the Society;

  (c) All money received by the Society by way of grants, gifts, donations, benefactions, bequests or transfer; and

  (d) All money received by the Society in any other manner or from any other sources.

(ii) The Fund shall deposit off moneys credited to the Society in such banks or to invest them in such manner as the Society may decide with the approval of the State Government.

(iii) The Fund shall meet expenses of the Society including expenses incurred in the exercise of its power and discharge of the functions out of the fund.

(iv) The Society shall prepare and maintain accounts and other relevant records and prepare an annual statement of accounts including the balance sheet of the Society in such forms as may be prescribed by the State Government.

(v) The Society shall forward annually to the State Government the accounts of the Society as certified by any authority as may be decided by the State Government.

5. RULES AND REGULATIONS OF THE SOCIETY

(i) The Society shall be known as "State Council of Vocational Training Society of ----------- State."

(ii) The address of the registered office of the Society shall be …………

(iii) The Society was formed on …………

(iv) The Society is within the jurisdiction of the Registrar of Societies,…………

(v) The business hours of the Society shall be between ………… a.m. to ………… p.m. on all working days except Sundays and government holidays.

(vi) These rules may be called "Rules of the Society—State Council of Vocational Training Society of ………… State."

(vii) The aims and main objects of the Society shall be as set out in the Memorandum of Association.

(viii) In these Rules and Regulations, the language shall be interpreted according to its ordinary meaning provided, however, unless the context necessarily indicates otherwise.

6. DEFINITIONS

For the purpose of these Rules and Memorandum of Association of the Society:

(i) "Rule" means any of the Rules, regulations and bye-laws of the Society, set out herein or in the Memorandum of Association.

(ii) 'Society' means the "State Council of Vocational Training Society of ………… State." as registered under …………

(iii) 'Act' means the ………… Societies Registration Act, (as relevant)

(iv) 'Governing Council' means Committee in terms of the ………… Societies Registration Act, ………… to which the management of the affairs of the Society "State Council of Vocational Training Society of ………… State." shall be entrusted.

(v) 'General Body' of the Society shall mean the body consisting of the members of the Governing Council together with other categories of members mentioned hereafter.

(vi) 'Chairperson' means the Chairperson of the Governing Council who shall also be the ex-officio President of the Society.

(vii) 'Annual General Meeting' means the meeting of the members of the Society held once in a year within six months after closing of the financial year of the Society for adopting the accounts of the Society, appointing auditors and discussing such other issues as may be brought before the meeting.

(viii) 'Registrar' means the Inspector General of Registration (as applicable under the relevant Act)

(ix) 'Special Resolution' means resolution passed by a majority of not less than three fourth of Society members present and entitled to vote as are present in person or by proxy at a General Body with a notice of not less than ………… days specifying the intention to propose the resolution as been duly given.

7. GENERAL BODY OF THE SOCIETY

(i) The General Body of the Society shall consist of a **two-tier structure**, one at the state level (Annexure–I) **termed Governing Body,** and another at the **Zonal level**, each consisting of more than seven members, selected/appointed by the State Government. The selected members may be experts in the relevant field and/or have significant experience in public life.

(ii) The Zonal-level Body must play a key role in collection of data relating to the training needs and requirements in their zone and must play an important role in the feedback mechanism. The recommendations of the Zonal-level Body must be forwarded to the State-level Body for consideration, before implementation.

(iii) The State-level Body may consider such recommendation from the Zonal-level Body, which again must be supported by two-thirds of it members.

(iv) The Society shall keep a roll of members with their addresses and occupations and every member shall sign the same.

(v) If a member of the Society changes his/her address, he/she shall notify his/her new address to the Secretary and the entry in the roll shall be changed accordingly. If such member fails to notify his/her address, the address in the rolls of the Society shall be deemed to be his/her address.

Membership of the Society

(i) When a person is appointed as a member of the Society by reason of the office of appointment he/she holds, his/her membership of the Society shall terminate when he/she ceases to hold that office or appointment. The respective parent organization shall, however, be entitled to remove their nominee at any time from membership of the Society and appoint others in his/her place.

(ii) A member of the Society shall hold the office for full tenure of the project.

(iii) A member of the Society shall lose his/her membership on the following grounds and reasons, and the Governing Council is empowered to take such decisions:

- (a) If he/she does not attend three consecutive meetings of the Society without sufficient cause or leave of absence granted to him/her by the Chairperson
- (b) If he/she dies, resigns, becomes of unsound mind or insolvent and is convicted of a criminal offence involving moral turpitude
- (c) If the tenure of his/her respective office as prescribed in these Rules and Regulations terminates
- (d) If he/she is a hindrance in the achievements of the aims and objects of the Society

(iv) The resignation of a member shall be tendered to the Society through the Member Secretary and shall not be effective till it has been accepted in writing by the Chairperson of the Governing Council on behalf of the Society

(v) A vacancy in the membership caused by any of the reasons mentioned above may be filled up by the Society

8. COMPOSITION OF THE GOVERNING COUNCIL AND TENURE OF OFFICE

Composition of the Governing Council

The Governing Council of the Society shall have the following members:

(i) Principal Secretary—Chairperson

(ii) Seniormost Technical Officer dealing with the Craftsmen Training/Skill Development in the State—Member Secretary

(iii) The members of the Governing Council shall consist of the following:

  (a) Three members nominated from Public Sector Units (Central/State)
  (b) One member nominated from DGE&T
  (c) One representative each from Government and Private ITIs
  (d) One representative from SCERT
  (e) Two nominees from the Trade Union
  (f) One nominee from the Skill Development Mission

Tenure of Office

(i) The tenure of the Governing Council shall be for a period of not more than three years, and the outgoing members shall be eligible for reappointment.

(ii) The ex-officio and nominated members of the Governing Council shall hold their office by virtue of being the nominees on behalf of their respective parent organizations. Their membership of the Governing Council shall automatically terminate in case they cease to be in that office or appointment by reason of which they hold membership in the Society or if they are removed by their respective nominating organization from membership of the Society. The respective nominating organization shall have power to nominate others as their representatives instead of the previous ones.

Termination of Membership

(i) The members of the Governing Council, except the ex-officio members, shall lose their membership on the following grounds, and the Governing Council is empowered to take such decision:

  (a) if they do not attend three consecutive meetings of the Governing Council without sufficient cause or leave of absence granted to them by the Chairperson;
  (b) If they resign, become of unsound mind or insolvent and are convicted of a criminal offence involving moral turpitude
  (c) If in the opinion of the Governing Council, continued association of any member is not conducive to the interest of the Society and an order in writing is made to that effect

(ii) Upon such termination of membership, the vacancies shall be filled in accordance with the relevant Rules and Regulations of the Society.

(iii) The resignation of a member of the Governing Council shall be tendered to the Secretary and shall not be effective till it has been accepted in writing by the Chairperson of the Governing Council on behalf of the Society.

(iv) The composition and tenure of the Zonal-level Council shall be defined by the Governing Council of the Society.

9. MEETINGS OF THE GOVERNING COUNCIL

(i) The meetings of the Governing Council shall be held as frequently as is considered necessary by the Chairperson but in any case not less than one meeting every three months for considering the progress of the Society, solving problems, if any, that may arise in the way of achieving the desired aims and objects as mentioned in the Memorandum of Association of the Society and planning future courses of action. However, during the first one year of the formation of the Society, when the process of upgradation of the ITI is underway, the Governing Council is expected to meet once every month.

(ii) The agenda for all meetings shall include confirmation of the minutes of the preceding meeting, which shall be prepared by the Secretary in consultation with Chairperson of the Society.

(a) Members of the Governing Council shall be served Notice in writing .... days before the date of all the meetings. The Chairperson shall have powers to reduce the notice period if the circumstances so warrant.

(b) The Notice of the meeting shall set out the date, time and venue of the proposed meeting of the Governing Council and shall be accompanied by the agenda of the meeting.

(c) Any accidental omission and/or non-receipt of the Notice for any meeting shall not itself invalidate the proceedings of any meeting of the Governing Council.

(iv) The Governing Council may frame such bye laws as it may deem necessary for holding and conducting its meetings.

(v) (a) The Chairperson shall preside over all the meetings of the Governing Council.

(b) If the Chairperson is unable to attend a meeting of the Governing Council, the Vice-Chairperson will preside over the meeting.

(c) If there is no Chairperson/Vice-Chairperson or the Chairperson/Vice-Chairperson is not present within half an hour of the time appointed for the meeting, the members present shall choose one of themselves to function as acting chairperson of that meeting.

(vi) (a) All questions in the meeting of the Governing Council where unanimity cannot be reached, shall be decided by a majority of votes.

(b) In case of equality of votes for and against a particular issue, the Chairperson shall have a casting vote in addition to his/her ordinary vote.

(vii) (a) The quorum for all the meetings of the Governing Council shall be one third of the total number of its members.

(b) Where the quorum is not present within half an hour after the time fixed for the meeting of the Governing Council, the meeting shall stand adjourned and may be held at the same place after half an hour following the adjournment. No quorum shall be necessary for such adjourned meeting.

(viii) The Chairperson of the Governing Council may himself/herself call or by resolution in writing signed by him/her require the Member Secretary to call a meeting of the Governing Council at any time.

10. POWERS, FUNCTIONS AND RESPONSIBILITIES OF THE GOVERNING COUNCIL

(i) With a view to attaining the aims and objects of the Society, the Governing Council shall discharge such duties and responsibilities, exercise such powers and undertake to carry out such activities as are considered essential in general and with particular reference to the following:

(a) To receive grants and contributions and to have custody of the funds of the Society

(b) To prepare the Budget estimates of the Society each year and sanction expenditure within the limits of the Budget approved by the Society at the Annual General Meeting

(c) To prepare and maintain accounts and other relevant records and annual statements of accounts including the Balance Sheet of the Society

(d) To fix, levy and receive such fees and other charges for service rendered by the Society

(e) To make, inform, adopt, amend, vary or rescind from time to time rules and bye-laws with the approval of General Body of the Society for regulation of any purpose connected with the management and administration of affairs of the Society and for the furtherance of its aims and objectives

(f) To perform such additional functions and carry out such duties as may from time to time be assigned to it by the Society

(g) To establish procedure in respect of services and technical advice to be rendered by the Society and the levy and collection of charges for the same

(h) To co-operate with any other organization in the matters of education, training, management and allied subjects

(i) To enter into arrangements for and on behalf of the Society

(j) To sue and defend all legal proceedings on behalf of the Society

(k) To appoint a committee or committees for disposal of any business of the Society or for advice in any matter pertaining to the Society

(l) To consider and pass such resolution on the annual report, the annual accounts and the financial estimates of the Society as it thinks fit

(m) To delegate to such extent it may deem necessary any of its powers to any officer or committee of the Governing Council

(n) To delegate powers as it may consider appropriate but not the powers for
- altering, extending or abridging the aims and objects of the Society;
- amalgamating either wholly or partially with any other Society having same or similar aims and objects;
- altering, extending or abridging the Rules and Regulations;
- making capital investment exceeding the approved Budget;
- borrowing money except for working capital exceeding the approved Budget;
- transferring by way of mortgage, pledge, hypothecation or otherwise any assets, movable or immovable, except as security for working capital;
- appointing bankers and auditors; and
- generally anything extraordinary and of major importance.

(ii) The Governing Council shall abide by any instructions issued by the Central Government in respect of any matter relating to implementation of NCVT guidelines.

(iii) (a) In the event of any matter not being provided for herein, the Governing Council has the power to make bye-laws, as it deems necessary, with the approval of the General Body of the Society.

(b) The Governing Council shall be the sole authority for resolving any doubts as to the interpretation of these provisions and its ruling shall be final and binding.

(iv) Subject to the provisions of the Act, no member of the Governing Council shall be held personally liable for any loss, damage or harm that may be caused by reason of any act or omission done by him/her in good faith, in course of discharging his/her functions and powers.

(v) No member of the Governing Council shall in that capacity be entitled to receive remuneration except travel allowance for attending the meeting, the quantum for which shall be fixed from time to time by the Governing Council with the approval of the Society.

11. AUTHORITIES OF THE SOCIETY

(i) The following shall be the authorities of the Society:

(a) The Chairperson of the Governing Council, who shall also be ex-officio President of the Society

(b) The Vice-Chairperson of the Governing Council, who shall also be the ex-officio Vice-President of the Society

(c) The Governing Council

(d) The Secretary of the Society who shall also be the ex-officio secretary of the Society and the Governing Council

(e) Such other authorities as may be constituted as such by the Governing Council

(ii) The Governing Council shall have powers to appoint financial and other committees/sub committees for carrying out the objects of the Society, and by resolution delegate to the committees or sub-committee(s) so constituted such of its powers for conduct of business as it may deem necessary.

12. THE CHAIRPERSON

(i) The Chairperson of the Governing Council shall be nominated by the Labour Minister/Principal Secretary of the State.

(ii) The Chairperson shall have the following powers, functions and responsibilities:

(a) The Chairperson may direct the Secretary to call a special meeting at a short notice in case of emergency.

(b) The Chairperson shall see that the affairs of the Society are run efficiently in accordance with the provisions of the Memorandum of Association, Rules and Regulations and bye-laws of the Society as may be framed.

(c) On such matters, which the Chairperson thinks are of sufficient importance and urgency and cannot wait for being placed in the next meeting of the Governing Council, and which he/she anticipates would get the approval of the Council, the Chairperson shall take decisions and place the same before the Governing Council at its next meeting.

(d) The Chairperson shall be the sole and absolute authority to judge the validity of the votes cast by the members of the Governing Council and General Body.

(e) The Chairperson may in writing delegate such of his/her powers as he/she may consider necessary to the Secretary.

(f) The Chairperson shall be entitled to invite any other person to attend the meeting of the Governing Council but such a person shall not have the power to vote.

(g) The Chairperson shall have the authority to review periodically the work and progress of the Society and to order inquiries into the affairs of the Society and to pass necessary orders on the recommendations of the inquiry committee.

(h) The Chairperson shall plan, direct and coordinate the overall working of the Society.

13. THE MEMBER SECRETARY

(i) (a) The Secretary shall be the Chief Executive Officer of the Society.

(b) The Secretary will be Member Secretary to the Society as well as the Governing Council and shall, in consultation with the Chairperson, prepare the agenda for the meetings of the General Body and Governing Council, convene such meetings, keep a true and accurate record of the proceedings of the same and forward all such documents, papers and related information as may be required in the discharge of his/her duties.

(ii) (a) The Secretary shall be charged with the responsibility of day-to-day management and administration of the Society.

(b) The Secretary shall perform his/her duties and functions and exercise his/her powers under the overall direction, superintendence and control of the Chairperson of the Governing Council under the Rules and Regulations of the Society.

(iii) In discharge of his/her functions, duties and powers, the Secretary, shall in particular do the following:

(a) Plan, direct, co-ordinate, organize and supervise day to day work of the Society
(b) Prepare concrete operational plan of action for the year, together with the revolving action plan for subsequent period of time to be determined by the Governing Council and budget estimates for the concerned period
(c) Report to the Governing Council on policy matters and achievements and delegate responsibilities to other officers, if required
(d) Present the report of the Governing Council in the annual general meeting of the Society
(e) Determine operational targets, measures and methods to achieve such targets and implement them after the approval of the Governing Council
(f) Submit the annual Budget of the succeeding year at least six months prior to the closing of the Financial Year and furnish the same to the State Government for getting funds from them, if any, after approval of the Governing Council
(g) Submit audited statements of accounts of the preceding year not later than three months after the close of the Financial Year
(h) Submit all such other reports as may be required by the Governing Council or otherwise
(i) Report to the Governing Council on all capital and recurring expenditure
(j) Sanction and incur expenditure in accordance with the procedure laid down in the bye-laws framed for the purpose and within the authority as may be delegated by the Governing Council
(k) Sign all deeds and documents for and on behalf of the Society
(l) Sign all documents and proceedings requiring authentication by the Society
(m) With the approval of the Governing Council, delegate any of his/her powers and functions and duties to any member staff of the Society/ITI which are not inconsistent with the provisions of these rules
(n) Do all such things as may be required for day-to-day management and administration of the Society

14. FUNDS OF THE SOCIETY

(i) The funds of the Society shall consist of the following:

(a) Fund received from the Central Government under the various Schemes
(b) Grants, contributions, and donations received by the Society from the Government of India, State Governments, Public Undertaking, private parties or any other sources
(c) Extra charges allowed to be collected by the State Government to the Society for any paid seats in the ITI for any training course

(ii) (a) The bankers of the Society shall be any nationalized bank having CBS facility
(b) All funds shall be paid into the Bank Account of the Society.

15. PROPERTY OF THE SOCIETY

(i) All the properties of the Society shall be acquired and registered in the name of the Society.
(ii) All funds and properties of the Society shall be used only for the aims and objects of the Society.

(iii) No property of the Society shall be disposed of except on the recommendations of the Governing Council. Disposal of any immovable property shall be approved by the Society as well.

16. ANNUAL REPORT

(i) A draft of Annual Report and the yearly accounts of the Society shall be prepared by the Secretary for consideration and approval of the Governing Council and shall thereafter be placed before the General Body at its Annual General Meeting for consideration and adoption;

(ii) Copies thereof, as finally approved by the Society, shall be supplied to the members of the Society.

(iii) The Books and Registers of the Society shall be kept ready for inspection by the Registrar at all reasonable hours.

17. SEAL OF THE SOCIETY

The Governing Council of the Society shall provide a seal and also its safe custody and the seal shall never be used except with the authority of Governing Council previously given and one member of the Council shall sign every instrument to which the seal is affixed and every such instrument shall be countersigned by the Secretary or by some other person appointed by the Council.

18. DISSOLUTION OF THE SOCIETY

The Society shall not be dissolved without the consent of the State Government and upon such dissolution, the assets of the Society shall be dealt within accordance with the provisions contained in the Societies Registration Act as applicable to the State of ____________.

19. SUBMISSION OF ANNUAL LIST

Once in every year, a list of members shall be filed with the Registrar of Societies as per provisions of (Section-----------) of the Societies Registration Act.

20. LEGAL PROCEEDINGS

The Society may sue or may be sued in the name of the Chairman or the Secretary of the Society as per provisions laid down under (Section----) of the Societies Registration Act.

21. APPLICABLITY CLAUSE

All the provisions of the Societies Registration Act, ------- shall apply to this Society.

22. POWERS OF THE GOVERNMENT

(i) The Central Government shall have the following powers in the conduct of the affairs of the Society:

   (a) To issue instructions for bringing about any changes in the Memorandum of Association and Rules and Regulation of the Society

(b) To call for such reports, documents and papers with respect to the activities of the Society as may be required from time to time

(c) To issue instructions regarding the utilization of the funds of the Society

(ii) The State Government shall have the following powers in the conduct of the affairs of the Society:

(a) To give directions as to the exercise of powers and performance of functions of the Society in matters involving substantial public interest, education and training policies.

(b) To evaluate from time to time the relevance, effectiveness, impact and efficiency of the Society in fulfilling its aims and objectives.

The above-mentioned powers will be exercised only on the recommendations of the NSC/SSC.

(iii) The State Government would not issue instruction which would contradict the instruction of Central Government.

23. RESTRICTIONS OF THE POWERS OF THE SOCIETY

The Society shall be precluded from making amends, varying, or rescinding such Rules and Regulations and bye-laws which provide for the prior approval of the Central Government or the State Government for doing or performing any act by the Society.

24. GENERAL

The Society shall function notwithstanding that any person who is entitled to be a member by reason of his office is not a member of the Society and notwithstanding any other vacancy in its body whether by non-appointment or otherwise and no act or proceedings of the Society or its Governing Council shall be deemed to be invalid merely for the reasons of any vacancy or defect in the constitution of the General Body, Governing Council or Committee as the case may be.

CERTIFIED THAT THIS IS THE CORRECT COPY OF THE RULES AND REGULATIONS OF THE SOCIETY.

Chairperson

Members of The Governing Council

Sl. No.	Name in Capital	Address	Occupation	Designation in the Society
01.				Chairman
02.				Vice Chairman
03.				Member Secretary
04.				Member
05.				Member
06.				Member
07.				Member
08.				Member

(Contd.)

Sl. No.	Name in Capital	Address	Occupation	Designation in the Society
09.				Member
10.				Member
11.				Member
12.				Member
13.				Member
14.				Member

Members of The Zonal Level Body

Sl. No.	Name in Capital	Address	Occupation	Designation in the Society
01.				Chairman
02.				Vice Chairman
03.				Member Secretary
04.				Member
05.				Member
06.				Member
07.				Member
08.				Member
09.				Member
10.				Member
11.				Member

Appendix II(A)

Sl. ....

DGE&T-19(22)/2010-CD date 5-10-10

Provisional National Trade Certificate (For Regular Candidates)

(Particulars of the State Directorate/DGE&T Offices)

PROVISIONAL NATIONAL TRADE CERTIFICATE

Shri/Shrimati/Kumar..Son/Wife/Daughter of Shri ....Roll No...............has completed the training programme at..(Name of Institute and Place) in ....trade. She/he was admitted during August/February.................session at SI. No. out of total.....................admitted against..............unit(s) affiliated to National Council for Vocational Training vide order No. DGE&T-........................dated. She/He has passed the All India Trade Test for Craftsmen Training Scheme held in the month of....................20.

Character during the period of training was found to be.....................

Trade Test Marks

Subject	Max. Marks	Marks obtained
1.		
2.		
3.		
4.		
5.		
Total		

Date of birth as recorded in the School Certificate.....................

Prepared by
Signature of Principal of ITI/
(In-charge, CTS of DGE&T Institute/with seal)

Checked by
(Facsimile Signature)
Secretary S.C.V.T./
Head of DGE&T Institute

(Signature of certificate holder)

Date ....

Appendix II(B)

Sl. ....

Provisional National Trade Certificate (for Private Candidates)

(Particulars of the State Directorate/DGE&T Offices)

PROVISIONAL NATIONAL TRADE CERTIFICATE

Shri/Shrimati/Kumari...Son/Wife/Daughter of Shri....................................Roll No.............having passed the prescribed trade test as PRIVATE candidate in the trade of ....held in the year of.........................20 is awarded this certificate provisionally.

The National Trade Certificate will be issued by the National Council for Vocational Training.

Trade Test Marks

S. No	Subject	Max. Marks*	Marks
1.			
2.			
3.			
4.			
5.			

*No sessional marks for private candidates

Date of Birth as recorded in the School Certificate..................

Prepared by:

Checked by

(Facsimile Signature)
Secretary, SCVT

(Signature of certificate holder)

Date..................

Appendix II(C)

Provisional National Trade Certificate (For BBBT)

Sl. ....

(Particulars of the State Directorate/DGE&T Offices)

PROVISIONAL NATIONAL TRADE CERTIFICATE

Shri/Shrimati/Kumari...............................Son/Wife/Daughterof Shri.................................... Roll No.........................having completed one year Broad Based Basic Training Course in the sector of _________at ....(Name of the institute and place) and passed the prescribed trade test held in ___________________20 is awarded this certificate provisionally.

The National Trade Certificate will be issued by the National Council for Vocational Training.

Period of training from .... to ....(Name of Institute and Place)

Character:

Trade Test Marks

Sl. No.	Subject	Written		Sessional		Total
		Max. Marks	Marks Obtained	Marks Obtained	Max. Marks	
1.	Trade Theory-1					
2.	Trade Theory-2					
3.	Practical-1					
4.	Practical-2					
5.	Workshop Cal. Science &Engg. Drg. OR Basic Computer Application					
6.	Entrepreneurship and Communication Skill					
	Grand Total					

Date of Birth as recorded in the School Certificate.............

Prepared By
Signature of Principal of ITI/
In-charge (with seal)

Checked by
Facsimile Sign of Secretary
State Council for Vocational Training

(Signature of certificate holder)

Date.............................

Appendix II(D)

Provisional National Trade Certificate (For Advanced Module)

Sl. ....

(Particulars of the State Directorate/DGE&T Offices)

PROVISIONAL NATIONAL TRADE CERTIFICATE

Shri/Shrimati/Kumari...........................Son/Wife/Daughter of Shri.. Roll No.........................having completed the six months Advanced Module (Name of the module) ...., in the sector of ____________at (Name of the institute) and passed the prescribed trade test held in the month of ________________, 20....... is awarded this certificate provisionally.

The National Trade Certificate will be issued by the National Council for Vocational Training.

Period of training from ....to ....

Character:

Trade Test Marks

Sl. No.	Subject for the Trade Test	Maximum Marks	Minimum Percentage of Marks	Minimum Marks Required for Passing (each subject)	Marks Obtained
1	Practical test Practical sessional	300 + 100 = total 400	60% in practical & aggregate	240	
2	Theory (written test) Theory (sessional work)	100 + 20 = total 120	40% in theory test & aggregate	48	

Date of Birth as recorded in the School Certificate....................................

Prepared By
Signature of Principal of ITI/
In-charge (with seal)

Checked by
Facsimile Signature of Secretary
State Council for Vocational Training

(Signature of certificate holder)

Date..............................

Appendix III(A)

National Trade Certificate (For Regular Candidates)

क्र.सं. (एन.टी.सी.)2008(S-8)
Sl.No.(N.T.C.)2008(S-8)

680001

भारत सरकार
GOVERNMENT OF INDIA
श्रम एवं रोजगार मंत्रालय
MINISTRY OF LABOUR AND EMPLOYMENT
राष्ट्रीय व्ययवसायिक प्रशिक्षण परिषद्
NATIONAL COUNCIL FOR VOCATIONAL TRAINING

राष्ट्रीय व्यवसाय प्रमाण–पत्र
NATIONAL TRADE CERTIFICATE

श्री / श्रीमति / कुमारी ....
सुपुत्र / पत्नी / सुपुत्री श्री .... को
.... में
प्रशिक्षण पूरा करने और माह .... सन् दो हजार ....
में आयाजित .... की निर्धारित व्यवसाय
परीक्षा में उतीर्ण होने पर यह व्यवसार प्रमाण–पत्र प्रदान किया जाता है।

Shri/Shrimati/Kumari ....
Son/Wife/Daughter of Shri ....
having completed the course of training at ....
.... *and passed the*
prescribed trade test in the trade of ....
held in the month of .... *two thousand* ....
is awarded this trade Certificate.

सचिव	सचिव
Secretary	Secretary
राष्ट्रीय व्यावसायिक प्रशिक्षण परिषद्	राज्य व्यावसायिक प्रशिक्षण परिषद्
National Council for Vocational Training	State Council for Vocational Training

प्रशिक्षण अवधि

.... से .... तक

Period of Training

From .... To ....

स्कूल के प्रमाण–पत्र में दर्ज जन्म–तिथि ....

Date of birth as recorded in School Certificate ....

पता ....

Address ....

प्रधानाचार्य ....

Principal ....

तारीख ....

Date ....

Appendix III(B)

National Trade Certificate (For Private Candidates)

क्र. सं. (एन. टी. सी.) (पी) 2008
Sl. No. –N.T.C. (P) 2008

06115

भारत सरकार
GOVERNMENT OF INDIA
श्रम एवं रोजगार मंत्रालय
MINISTRY OF LABOUR AND EMPLOYMENT
राष्ट्रीय व्ययवसायिक प्रशिक्षण परिषद्
NATIONAL COUNCIL FOR VOCATIONAL TRAINING

राष्ट्रीय व्यवसाय प्रमाण–पत्र
NATIONAL TRADE CERTIFICATE

(प्राईवेट उम्मीदवार)
(PRIVATE CANDIDATE)

श्री / श्रीमति / कुमारी .... सुपुत्र / पत्नी / सुपुत्री श्री .... को .... सन् दो हजार .... में आयोजित .... की निर्धारित व्यवसाय परीक्षा में उतीर्ण होने पर यह व्यवसाय प्रमाण–पत्र प्रदान किया जाता है।

Shri/Shrimati/Kumari .... Son/Wife/ Daughter of Shri .... having passed the prescribed trade test in the trade of .... held in .... Two Thousand .... is awarded this Trade Certificate.

सचिव
Secretary
राष्ट्रीय व्यावसायिक प्रशिक्षण परिषद्
National Council for Vocational Training

सचिव
Secretary
राज्य व्यावसायिक प्रशिक्षण परिषद्
State Council for Vocational Training

Appendix III(C)

National Trade Certificate (For BBBT)

क्र. सं. सी. ओ. ई. (बी. बी. बी. टी.) 2008
Sl. No. C.O.E. (B.B.B.T.) 2008

No. 024331

भारत सरकार
GOVERNMENT OF INDIA
श्रम एवं रोजगार मंत्रालय
MINISTRY OF LABOUR AND EMPLOYMENT
राष्ट्रीय व्ययवसायिक प्रशिक्षण परिषद्
NATIONAL COUNCIL FOR VOCATIONAL TRAINING

राष्ट्रीय व्यवसाय प्रमाण–पत्र
NATIONAL TRADE CERTIFICATE

श्री / कुमारी / श्रीमती ....
सुपुत्र / सुपुत्री / पत्नी / श्री ....
को .... क्षेत्र में
एक वर्षीय व्यापक आधारित बुनियादी प्रशिक्षण पाठ्यक्रम पूरा करने के पश्चात् और ....
सन् दो हजार .... में आयोजित निर्धारित व्यवसाय परीक्षा उतीर्ण करने पर यह व्यवसाय प्रमाण–पत्र प्रदान किया जाता है।

Shri/Km/Smt .... Son/Daughter/
Wife of Shri ....
having completed one year Broad Based Basic Training Course in the Sector of ....
....
at .... and passed the prescribed Trade Test
held in .... two thousand ....
is awarded this Trade Certificate.

सचिव
Secretary
राज्य व्यावसायिक प्रशिक्षण परिषद्
State Council for Vocational Training

सचिव
Secretary
राष्ट्रीय व्यावसायिक प्रशिक्षण परिषद्
National Council for Vocational Training

प्रशिक्षण की अवधि .... से .... तक

Period of Training From .... To ....

क्षेत्रः ....

Sector: ....

आठ सप्ताह की अवधि वाले प्रत्येक बुनियादी मॉड्यूल:

Basic Modules each of eight week duration:

1.
2.
3.
4.
5.
6.

जेनेरिक मॉड्यूल: ....

Generic Module: ....

स्कूल प्रमाण–पत्र में दर्ज जन्म तिथि: ....

Date of Birth as recorded in School Certificate: ....

पता: ....

Address: ....

प्रधानाचार्य: ....

Principal: ....

दिनांक: ....

Date: ....

Appendix III(D)

National Trade Certificate (For Advanced Modules) +36

क्र. सं. सी. ओ. ई. (ए. टी. एम.) / 2008
Sl. No. C.O.E. (A.T.M.)/2008

No. 015956

भारत सरकार
GOVERNMENT OF INDIA
श्रम एवं रोजगार मंत्रालय
MINISTRY OF LABOUR AND EMPLOYMENT
राष्ट्रीय व्ययवसायिक प्रशिक्षण परिषद्
NATIONAL COUNCIL FOR VOCATIONAL TRAINING

राष्ट्रीय व्यवसाय प्रमाण–पत्र

NATIONAL TRADE CERTIFICATE

श्री / कुमारी / श्रीमति ....
सुपुत्र / सुपुत्री / पत्नी श्री ....
को .... (संस्थान का नाम)
से .... क्षेत्र में .... में
छह माह का उच्च मॉड्यूल पूरा करने के पश्चात् तथा .... 20 ....
में आयोजित निर्धारित व्यवसाय परीक्षा उतीर्ण करने पर यह राष्ट्रीय व्यवसाय प्रमाण–पत्र प्रदान किया जाता है।

Shri/Km./Smt. ....
Son/Daughter/Wife of Shri .... having completed
the six months Advanced Module of ....
in the .... Sector at ....
.... (Name of the Institute)
and passed the prescribed Trade Test held in .... 20 ....
is awarded this National Trade Certificate.

सचिव
Secretary
राज्य व्यावसायिक प्रशिक्षण परिषद
State Council for Vocational Training

सचिव
Secretary
राष्ट्रीय व्यावसायिक प्रशिक्षण परिषद्
National Council for Vocational Training

प्रशिक्षण की अवधि .... से .... तक

Period of Training From .... To ....

स्कूल प्रमाण–पत्र मे दर्ज जन्म तिथि : ....

Date of Birth as recorded in the School Certificate: ....

पता : ....

Address: ....

प्रधानाचार्य : .... मोहर ....

Principal .... Stamp ....

दिनांक : ....

Date: ....

Appendix III(E)

National Trade Certificate
(For Specialised Modules)

Sl. ....
Code No. ....

GOVERNMENT OF INDIA
MINISTRY OF LABOUR & EMPLOYMENT
NATIONAL COUNCIL FOR VOCATIONAL TRAINING
NATIONAL TRADE CERTIFICATE

This is to certify that Shri/Shrimati/Kumari .... Son/Wife/Daughter of Shri ....has successfully completed the six months Training Course in Specialized Module * Name of the Module* in the............................ Sector at................................(Name of the institute)... from ....to......................and passed the prescribed Trade Test held in ______________________________two thousand __________

Secretary
State Council for Vocational Training

Authorised Signature & Seal of Industry Partner

PS:

1. This certificate has the recognition of National Council for Vocational Training vide letter No DGE&T 19(2)/2007-CD, 27.6.2008.
2. Pre requisite qualifications for this certificate are National Trade Certificate/National Trade Certificate of Broad Based Basic Training in ....Sector and National Trade Certificate of Advanced Module in ....of...........Sector .

On Reverse side

Father's Name:

Date of Birth as recorded in School Certificate

APPENDIX IV

Recognition of Trade Certificates Awarded by Various Authorities at the Level of Craftsmen

No. TC/NCT-14(5)/66

GOVERNMENT OF INDIA
DIRECTORATE GENERAL OF EMPLOYMENT AND TRAINING
MINISTRY OF LABOUR
Shram Shakti Bhawan, Rafi Marg, New Delhi 110001

Dated 26th Dec. 1966

MEMORANDUM

Subject: Recognition of the trade certificates awarded by the various authorities to the trainees of the training institutes run by them for the training of persons at the level of Craftsmen.

1. The Ministry of Home Affairs, etc. are aware that the Ministry of Labour, Employment and Rehabilitation is concerned with the recognition of certificates awarded at the level of craftsmen for the purpose of recruitment to the posts and services under the Central Government for which a diploma/certificate in craftsmanship or a National Trade Certificates is prescribed as the requisite qualification. Under the Craftsmen Training Scheme and the Apprenticeship Training Scheme, under the Apprentices Act 1961 of this Ministry's National Trade Certificates and National Apprenticeship Certificates, which are issued by the National Council for Training in Vocational Trades, now National Council for Vocational Training (NCVT), after all-India tests to the trainees of the industrial training institutes and the apprentices are both recognized for the purposes of employment as stated above. A list of trades under the Craftsmen Training Scheme and the Apprenticeship Training Scheme under the Apprentices Act 1961 is enclosed for ready reference.
2. The trades/courses run by the different ministries/departments, etc. which are in line with the trades/courses conducted by the Directorate General of Employment and Training may be affiliated to the National Council for Training in Vocational Trades for the purpose of recognition.
3. The Ministry has been receiving references from different ministries and departments regarding the recognition of certificates awarded by them to the trainees of the training institutes run by them in trades or courses other than those included in the Directorate General of Employment and Training Programme. It has been decided that trade certificates in trades other than those included in the Directorate General of Employment and Training programme awarded by different ministries, departments, etc. may also be recognized by this Ministry. The enclosed note outlines the procedure to be followed for the purpose of recognition of the trade certificates by this Ministry.

Sd/- G Jagannathan
Under Secretary to the Government of India

To,
All Ministries of the Government of India and their various Departments, Department of Parliamentary Affairs, Lok Sabha Secretariat, Rajya Sabha Secretariat, President's Secretariat, Prime Minister's Secretariat, Supreme Court, Comptroller and Auditor General of India, Department of Atomic Energy, DGE&T, New Delhi, CPWD, (New Delhi), Central Water and Power Commission, UPSC, UGC, (New Delhi), Planning Commission, Election Commission, Programme Evaluation Organisation and Committee on Plan Projects, Planning Commission.

Copy, with enclosures forwarded to:

1. Principal Information Officer, Press Information Bureau with the request that a press note explaining the above decision in suitable terms may kindly be issued as soon as possible.
2. All State Governments and administrations of Union Territories for favour of issue of similar instructions at an early date
3. Principals of all (i) Central Training Institute for Instructors, (ii) Industrial Training Institutes under the CTI and those affiliated to the NCVT.
4. All State Directors concerned with Training of Craftsmen/Directors of National Employment Service.
5. Shri M L Salhotra, T C Section for issuing an amendment to the Craftsmen Training Manual.
6. EEI Section for providing this to all Employment Exchanges, etc.

DIRECTORATE GENERAL OF EMPLOYMENT AND TRAINING, MINISTRY OF LABOUR NEW DELHI

Procedure to be followed by the different Ministries, Government Departments, etc. in connection with the recognition of certificates awarded by them at the level of Craftsmen (other than Degree and Diploma level) to the trainees of the training institutes run by them.

Background Information

The Ministry of Labour is concerned with the recognition of technical and professional qualifications at the level of craftsmen for recruitment to the posts and services under the services under the Government of India for which a Diploma/Certificate in craftsmanship or a National Trade Certificate is prescribed as the requisite qualification. Accordingly, diplomas and certificates issued by different authorities at the level of craftsmen should be recognized by that ministry. The Directorate General of Employment and Training in the Ministry of Labour, Employment and Rehabilitation has a number of training schemes which cover a number of engineering and non-engineering trades for the purpose of imparting training at the level of craftsmen. The Industrial Training Institutes which are functioning under the Craftsmen Training Scheme of the Directorate General of Employment and Training conduct courses in 43 engineering trades and 24 non-engineering trades, and training is imparted according to the standards recommended by the National Council for Vocational Training. National Trade Certificates which are issued to the trainees by the National Council for Vocational Training after an All India Trade Test are recognized by this ministry for employment to the posts and services under the Government of India as stated above. Similarly, the National Apprenticeship Certificates which are issued by the NCVT to the apprentices after completion of the Apprentices Act 1961 are recognized for the purpose of recruitment to the posts and service under the Government of India. The number of trades which have been designated under the Apprentices Act is 137 at present.

Different Ministries/Government Departments are running their own training schemes in the same trades which are included in the DGE&T training schemes and following standards laid down by the National Council for Vocational Training. Such training schemes may be affiliated to the National Council for the purpose of recognition of the certificates awarded by them. Where, however, the trades/courses are not included in the DGE&T training programme, the certificates awarded by them in respect of such trades/ courses have not been recognized by this ministry so far.

Procedure to be followed

It has now been decided that the certificates awarded in trades/courses which are conducted at the level of craftsmen by the different Ministries/Departments in trades/courses other than those included in the DGE&T, the training programme should be recognized for the purposes of employment as stated above. For this purpose, the procedure as indicated below should be followed by the Ministry/Government Department concerned:

1. The syllabus for the practical training and theoretical instructions should be drafted by experts in the trade and finalized in consultation with a committee of experts in the trade. The list of tools and equipment required for the purpose of training to cover the syllabus should also be drafted.
2. The educational qualification for admission, the age limit, etc. should be suggested in the draft.
3. A committee consisting of a few experts, say five or six, who have knowledge and experience in the trade should be constituted, to examine the syllabus, list of tools and equipment, etc.
4. A scheme for training according to the syllabus should be drafted indicating the time of admission, number of trainees to be admitted, the ratio of instructor/teacher to the trainees, location to the institute, the method of keeping progress records, the method of conducting the final trade test, the certificate to be awarded in the trade, etc.
5. The scheme mentioned above, together with the syllabus and other training standards recommended by the committee of experts (which may be called Trade Committee), should be sent to the DGE&T for the purpose of recognition of the certificate at the level of craftsmen.
6. The DGE&T would examine the training programme with a view to find out whether the course concerned is at the level of craftsmen and training standards have been approved by a committee of experts appointed by the Ministry/Department concerned for the purpose.
7. The Ministry/Department concerned, thereafter will be intimated regarding the recognition of the certificate which may be awarded after a necessary test conducted by them for the purpose of recruitment to the posts under the Central Government subject to the fulfillment of the above-mentioned conditions.

List (as on 20-5-68) of Trades under CTS of the DGE&T in Respect of Which Diplomas/Certificate Awarded from Time to Time have been Recognized by the Government of India

NON-ENGINEERING TRADES

1. Bleaching, Dyeing and Calico Printing
2. Book Binding
3. Cane, Willow and Bamboo Work
4. Cutting and Tailoring
5. Cutting and Tailoring (Men)
6. Cutting and Tailoring (Women)
7. Confectionery and Bakery (including Preservation of Fruits)
8. Coir Weaving
9. Embroidery and Needlework
10. Embroidery and Needlework (including Salma,Tila and Lamp and Lampshade Work)
11. Fret Work and Manufacture of Wooden Toys
12. Carbo Spinning
13. Hand Composing and Proof Reading
14. Hand Weaving of Fancy and Furnishing Fabrics
15. Hand Weaving of Niwar, Tapes, Durries and Carpets
16. Hand Weaving of Woolen Fabrics
17. Knitting with Hand Machine
18. Manufacture of Footwear
19. Manufacture of Household Utensils
20. Manufacture of Sports Goods (Leather)
21. Manufacture of Sports Goods (Misc.)
22. Manufacture of Sports Goods (Wood)
23. Manufacture of Suitcases and other Leather Goods
24. Preservation of Fruits and Vegetables and Manufacture of Confectionery
25. Preservation of Fruits and Vegetables
26. Printing Machine Operator
27. Stenography (English)
28. Stenography (Hindi)
29. Signaller (Railways)
30. Weaving of Silk and Woolen Fabrics
31. Wood Turning and Lacquer Work
32. *Wood Carving and Inlaying

* only Diplomas in Craftsmanship awarded.

ENGINEERING TRADES

1. Blacksmith
2. Building Constructor
3. Carpenter
4. Clock and Watch Repairer
5. Die Fitter
6. Draughtsman (Civil)
7. Draughtsman (Mechanical)
8. Electrician
9. Electroplater
10. Fitter
11. Grinder
12. Lineman and Wireman
13. Mechanic (Dom. Ref)
14. Mechanic (Instrument)
15. Mechanic (I.C. Engines)
16. Mechanic (Motor)
17. Mechanic (Radio)
18. Mechanic (Tractor)
19. Mechanic (Motor Vehicle)
20. Mechanic (Radio and Television)
21. Mechanic (Diesel)
22. Mechanic (General)
23. Machinist
24. Machinist (Grinder)
25. Machinist (Miller)
26. Machinist (Shaper, Slotter and Planer)
27. Moulder
28. Painter and Decorator
29. Pattern Maker
30. Plumber
31. Painter
32. Mechanic (Refrigeration and Air Conditioning)
33. Sheet Metal Worker
34. Surveyor
35. Tool Maker
36. Turner
37. Upholstery
38. Welder (Gas and Electric)
39. Wireless Operator
40. Wireman
41. Watch and Clock Maker

Appendix V

Survey of Occupations around ITIs for Determining the Scope for Training in the ITIs (Industry-wise Survey)

The following points may have to be taken into consideration while deciding to introduce the trades or suggesting the closure of the unpopular trades and substituting them with more popular trades:

1. Whether the skills of the trades require institutional training
2. Whether the trades can be taught in their entirety in the ITIs
3. Whether the persons trained in these trades can secure employment
4. Whether the joint effort of the ITIs and the industry would constitute the training programme
5. Whether the occupations can be learnt in shorter periods of time and do we actually call such occupation as trades or operations and are they worth introducing in the ITIs

With the above criteria in view, it would thereafter be necessary to conduct area-wise and industry-wise surveys of the occupations in order to assess the demand and supply position.

These surveys may secure information in regard to the following:

1. Total number of skilled and semi-skilled workers employed
2. The number employed each year
3. Probable number required in coming 5 to 10 years
4. The trades in which training is required
5. General education requirements of the trades
6. Wage rate of skilled and semi-skilled workers
7. Opportunities of joint training facilities in the industry and the ITIs
8. Physical requirements for employment and such other information that would be helpful in organizing the training courses

After having decided the trades for which the training in the ITIs would be beneficial, the next step to be decided would be

1. Whether the trade is one of the existing trades under CTS, and if so,

(i) Do we need to provide additional seats in the trade?
(ii) Can we run these seats in shifts by utilizing the equipment provided for the trainees in the first shift?
(iii) Do we need to discontinue the trade and substitute it with popular trades?

2. If the trade does not exists under CTS Is the trade meant for the local employment market or does its utility exist elsewere in the district/state/country?

(i) Is the equipment easily available?
(ii) What would be the duration of such courses?
(iii) What would be the education requirement of the candidates seeking admission in the new trade?
(iv) Are the industries willing to offer their experts for designing the syllabi and list of tools which ultimately would be examined and accepted by NCVT for adoption for the purpose of examination/certification and recognition?
(v) What is the wage rate of skilled and semi-skilled workers?

(vi) Would it be possible to introduce the trade in the ITIs?
(vii) Can the trade be taught by the joint effort of the ITIs and industries?
(viii) Is there any foreign-exchange component in the equipment required to teach the skills of the trades? If so, what would be the quantum of such components?

Proforma for Conducting Industry Survey in Trades in which there is Absolute Employment Potential in the Area

Name of the proposed trades	Total no. of semi-skilled and skilled workers employed	No. of semi-skilled and skilled employed each year	General education standard of workers	Wage rate	Probable no. required in the coming 5 to 10 years	Is it advisable to introduce the trades in ITIs?	Is it necessary to have an apprenticeship programme?
1.	2	3	4	5	6	7	8

Proforma Suggested for Submitting Proposals for Discontinuance of Unpopular Trades and Substituting them with Popular Tardes Out of Existing NCVT Trades

Summary of Trades to be Abolished/ Introduced

Sl. No.	Name of the trade	Seat sanctioned	Trainees on roll	Seats to be abolished	Seats to be introduced	Ultimate total seating capacity
1	2	3	4	5	6	7
(Engineering Trades— 2 years' Course)						
1.						
2.						
3.						
4.						
5.						
6.						
7.						
8.						
9.						
10.						
11.						
12.						
13.						
14.						

(Contd.)

Sl. No.	Name of the trade	Seat sanctioned	Trainees on roll	Seats to be abolished	Seats to be introduced	Ultimate total seating capacity
1	2	3	4	5	6	7
(Engineering Trades—1-year Course)						
1.						
2.						
3.						
4.						
5.						
6.						
7.						
8.						
(Non-Engineering Trades—1-year Course)						
1.						
2.						
3.						
4.						
5.						
6.						
7.						
8.						

Name of the trade/s	Seats to be abolished	Name of the trade/s	Seats to be introduced

Certificates To Be Furnished

- Value of equipment/hand tools/furniture rendered surplus and action suggested for disposal/ utilization/transfer to other ITIs.
- Value of equipment/hand tools/furniture required for the suggested trades and amount required for procurement.
- Whether funds are available or not
- Whether accommodation is adequate
- Whether the non-recurring grant exceeds the sanctioned amount
- Action suggested for the disposal of surplus instructional staff. The proposed change should not enhance the number of seats sanctioned at the ITIs.

Information may be sent by email at **secretaryncvt@nic.in**

Appendix VI

Organisation Chart of an Industrial Training Institute

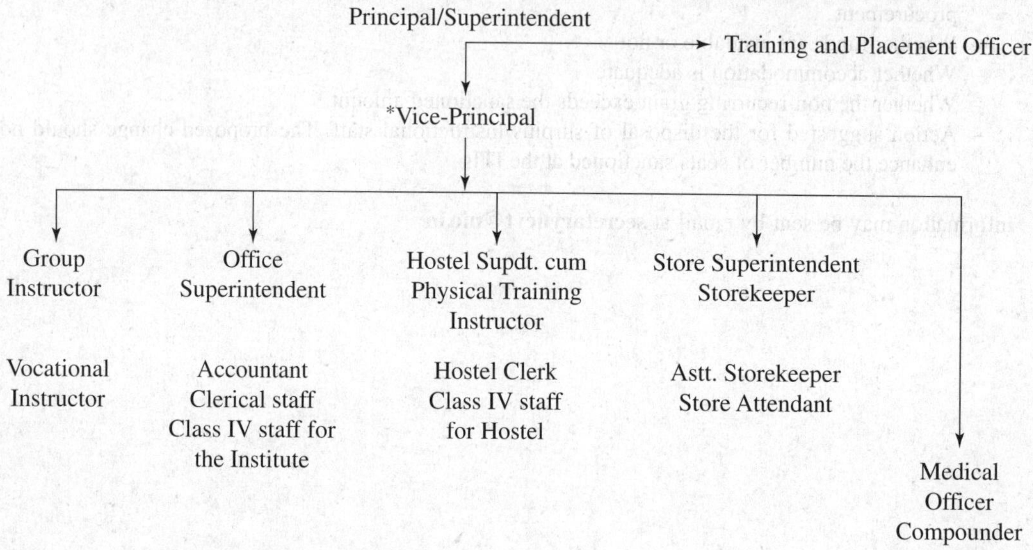

Instructor for Allied trades
Drawing Instructor
Millwright Instructor
Mathematics Instructor
AV Instructor
Workshop Attendant
Supporting Staff

* Wherever sanctioned

Appendix VII

List of Engineering and Non-Engineering Trades under the Craftsmen Training Scheme as on 26.12.2013

1. Engineering Trades

S. No.	Name of the Trade	Duration	Entry Qualification	Syllabus Revised During the Year	Trade Introduced During the Year
1.	Architectural Assistant	1 year	Passed 10th class examination with 40% marks in Mathematics or Secondary Standard under 10+2 system of education or its equivalent.		2003
2.	Attendant Operator (Chemical Plant)	(a) 2 years (b) 6 months	Passed 10th class examination under 10+2 system of education with Physics, Chemistry and Mathematics as one of the subjects or its equivalent. Passed BSc with Physics and Chemistry.	2010	
3.	Building Maintenance	6 months	Passed 10th class examination under 10+2 system of education or its equivalent.		2003
4.	Carpenter	1 year	Passed 8th class examination under 10+2 system of education with Science as one of the subjects or its equivalent.		
5.	Draughtsman (Civil)	2 years	Passed 10th class examination under 10+2 system of education with Science and Mathematics or its equivalent.	2007	
6.	Draughtsman (Mechanical)	2 years	Passed 10th class examination under 10+2 system of education with Science and Mathematics or its equivalent.	2007	
7.	Electrician	2 years	Passed 10th class examination under 10+2 system of education with Science as one of the subjects or its equivalent.	2007	
8.	Electronic Mechanic	2 years	Passed Matriculation examination under 10+2 system of education with Science and Mathematics or its equivalent.	2005	
9.	Electroplater	2 years	Passed 10th class examination under 10+2 system of education or its equivalent.	1999	
10.	Fitter	2 years	Passed 10th class examination under 10+2 system of education or its equivalent.	2007	
11.	Foundryman	1 year	Passed class 8th examination under 10+2 system of education or its equivalent.	1998	
12	Goldsmith	1 year	Passed 8th class examination under 10+2 system of education or its equivalent		2010

(*Contd.*)

S. No.	Name of the Trade	Duration	Entry Qualification	Syllabus Revised During the Year	Trade Introduced During the Year
13.	Information Technology and Electronics System Maintenance	2 years	Passed 10th class examination under 10+2 system of education with Science. *Desirable*—12th class pass with Mathematics and Physics.	2007	
	Instrument Mechanic	2 years	Passed 10th class examination under 10+2 system of education with Science as one of the subjects or its equivalent.	2000	
15.	Instrument Mechanic (Chemical Plant)	(a) 2 years (b) 6 months	Passed 10th class examination under 10+2 system of education with Physics, Chemistry and Mathematics as one of the subjects or its equivalent. Passed BSc with Physics and Chemistry.	2002 2010	2002
16.	Interior Decoration and Designing	1 year	Passed 10th class examination under 10+2 system of education.		2003
17.	Laboratory Assistant (Chemical Plant)	(a) 2 years (b) 6 months	Passed 10th class examination under 10+2 system of education with Physics, Chemistry and Mathematics as one of the subjects or its equivalent. Passed BSc with Physics and Chemistry.	2010	2003
18.	Lift Mechanic	2 years	Passed 10th class examination under 10+2 system of education with Science or its equivalent.		2003
19.	Machinist	2 years	Passed 10th class examination under 10+2 system of education or its equivalent.	2007	
20.	Machinist (Grinder)	2 years	Passed 10th class examination under 10+2 system of education or its equivalent.	1997	
21.	Maintenance Mechanic (Chemical Plant)	2 years	Passed 10th class examination with Physics, Chemistry and Mathematics under 10+2 system of education or its equivalent.	2010	2003
22.	Marine Fitter	2 years	Passed 10th class examination under 10+2 system of education with 50% marks in Mathematics and Science or its equivalent.	2010	2005
23.	Mason (Building Constructor)	1 year	Passed 8th class examination under 10+2 system of education or its equivalent.	2004	
24.	Mech. Communication Equipment Maintenance	1 year	Passed 10th class examination under 10+2 system of education or its equivalent		2006
25.	Mech. Repair and Maintenance of Heavy Vehicles	1 year	Passed 10th class examination under 10+2 system of education or its equivalent		2006
26.	Mech. Repair and Maintenance of Light Vehicles	1 year	Passed 10th class examination under 10+2 system of education or its equivalent		2006
27.	Mech. Repair and Maintenance of Two Wheelers	6 months	Passed 10th class examination under 10+2 system of education or its equivalent.		2006

(Contd.)

S. No.	Name of the Trade	Duration	Entry Qualification	Syllabus Revised During the Year	Trade Introduced During the Year
28.	Mechanic (Diesel)	1 year	Passed 10th class examination under 10+2 system or its equivalent.	1998	
29.	Mechanic (Motor Vehicle)	2 years	Passed 10th class examination under 10+2 system of education with Science as one of the subjects or its equivalent.	2002	
30.	Mechanic (Radio and TV)	2 years	Passed 10th class examination under 10+2 system of education with Science as one of the subject or its equivalent.	1996	
31.	Mechanic (Refrigeration and Air Conditioner)	2 years	Passed 10th class examination under 10+2 system of education with Science and Mathematics or its equivalent.	2002	
32.	Mechanic (Tractor)	1 year	*Essential*—Passed 8th class examination under 10+2 system of education or its equivalent. *Desirable*—Passed 10th class examination under 10+2 system of education with science (Physics and Chemistry) as one of the subjects or its equivalent.	1996	
33.	Mechanic (Agricultural Machinery)	2 years	*Essential*—Passed 8th class examination under 10+2 system of education or its equivalent. *Desirable*—Passed 10th class examination under 10+2 system of education with Science (Physics and Chemistry) as one of the subjects.		
34.	Mechanic (Auto, Electrical and Electronics)	6 months	Passed 10th class examination under 10+2 system of education with Science and Mathematics or its equivalent.		2003
35.	Mechanic Computer Hardware	2 years	Passed 10+2 or Intermediate or Pre-university with Physics as one of the subject.		2003
36.	Mechanic Consumer Electronics	2 years	Passed 10th class examination under 10+2 system of education with Mathematics and Science or its equivalent.		2003
37	Mechanic Industrial Electronics	2 years	Passed 12th class examination with Physics, Chemistry and Mathematics.		2003
38.	Mechanic Lens/Prism Grinding	1 year	Passed 10th class examination under 10+2 system of education or its equivalent.		2006
39.	Mechanic Machine Tools Maintenance	3 years	Matriculation with Science and Mathematics or its equivalent.	1999	
40.	Mechanic Mechatronics	2 years	Passed 10+2 examination with Physics, Chemistry and Mathematics.		2003
41.	Mechanic Medical Electronics	2 years	Passed 10th class examination under 10+2 system of education with Mathematics and Science or its equivalent.		2003

(*Contd.*)

S. No.	Name of the Trade	Duration	Entry Qualification	Syllabus Revised During the Year	Trade Introduced During the Year
42.	Mechanic-cum-Operator Electronics Communication System	2 years	Passed 10th class examination under 10+2 system of education with Science as one of the subjects or its equivalent.	2002	
43.	Operator Advanced Machine Tools	2 years	Passed 12th class examination with Physics, Chemistry and Mathematics.		2003
44.	Painter General	2 years	Passed 8th class examination or its equivalent.		
45.	Physiotherapy Technician	1 year	Passed 12th class examination under 10+2 system of education with Physics, Chemistry and Biology.		2006
46.	Plastic Processing Operator	1 year	Passed 10th class examination under 10+2 system of education or its equivalent.		
47.	Plumber	1 year	Passed 8th class examination under 10+2 system of education or its equivalent.	2004	
48.	Pump Operator-cum-Mechanic	1 year	Passed 10th class examination under 10+2 system of education with Science or its equivalent.	2007	
49.	Radiology Technician (Radio Diagnosis and Radiotherapy)	2 years	Passed 12th class examination Under 10+2 system of education with Physics, Chemistry and Biology.		2006
50.	Sanitary Hardware fitter	6 months	Passed 8th class examination under 10+2 system of education or its equivalent.		2003
51.	Sheet Metal Worker	1 year	Passed 8th class examination under 10+2 system of education or its equivalent.	1996	
52.	Spinning Technician	2 years	Passed 10th class examination		2007
53.	Surveyor	2 years	Passed 10th class examination under 10+2 system of education with Science and Mathematics or its equivalent.	2007	
54.	Textile Mechatronics	2 years	Passed 10th class examination		2007
55.	Textile Wet Processing Technician	1 year	Passed 10th class examination under 10+2 system of education with Science and Mathematics or its equivalent.	2007	
56.	Tool and Die Maker (Dies and Moulds)	3 years	Passed 10th class examination under 10+2 system of education with Science or its equivalent.	2007	
57.	Tool and Die Maker (Press Tools, Jigs and Fixtures)	3 years	Passed 10th class examination under 10+2 system of education with Science or its equivalent.	2007	
58.	Turner	2 years	Passed 10th class examination under 10+2 system of education or its equivalent.	2007	
59.	Vessel Navigator	2 years	Passed 10th class examination under 10+2 system of education with 50% marks in Mathematics and Science or its equivalent	2010	2005
60.	Welder (Gas and Electric)	1 year	Passed 8th class examination under 10+2 system of education or its equivalent.	2005	

(Contd.)

S. No.	Name of the Trade	Duration	Entry Qualification	Syllabus Revised During the Year	Trade Introduced During the Year
61.	Weaving Technician	2 years	Passed 10th class examination under 10+2 system of education with Mathematics and Science or its equivalent		2007
62.	Wireman	2 years	Passed 8th class examination or its equivalent.	1996	
63.	Marine Engine Fitter	1 year	Passed 10th class examination or its equivalent.		2010
64.	Domestic Painter	1 years	Passed 10th class examination under 10+2 system of education.		2012
65.	Industrial Painter	1 year	Passed 10th class under 10+2 system of education		2012
66.	Rubber Technician	1 year	Passed 10th class examination		2012
67.	Mechanic Mining Machinery	2 years	Passed 12th class with Science		2012
68.	Stone Mining Machine Operator	1 years	Passed 10th class under 10+2 system		
69.	Stone Processing Machines Operator	1 year	Passed 10th class under 10+2 system		2013
70.	Excavator Operator (Mining)	6 months	8th class Passed		2013

2. Non-Engineering Trades

S. No.	Name of the Trade	Duration	Entry Qualification	Syllabus Revised During the Year	Trade Introduced During the Year
1.	Baker and Confectioner	1 year	Passed 10th class examination under 10 + 2 system of education or its equivalent.		
2.	Cabin/Room Attendant	6 months	i) Passed 10th Class Examination under 10+2 System of Education. ii) Working knowledge of English and Hindi.		2003
3.	Cane Willow and Bamboo Work	1 Year	Passed 8th class or its equivalent.		
4.	Computer Aided Embroidery and Needle work	6 months	Passed Class 10th examination under 10+2 system of education or its equivalent		2006
5.	Computer Operator and Programming Assistant	1 year	Passed 10th class	2012	2003
6.	Corporate Housekeeping	6 months	Passed 10th class examination under 10+2 system of education.		2003
7.	Craftsman Food Production (General)	1 year	Passed 10th class exam under 10+2 system of education or its equivalent.		1998

(*Contd.*)

S. No.	Name of the Trade	Duration	Entry Qualification	Syllabus Revised During the Year	Trade Introduced During the Year
8.	Craftsman Food Production (Vegetarian)	1 year	Passed 10th class examination under 10+2 system of education or its equivalent.		1998
9.	Crèche Management	6 months	Passed 10th class examination under 10+2 system of education		2003
10.	Cutting and Sewing	1 Year	Passed 8th class or its equivalent.	2002	
11.	Dairying	1 year	Passed 10th class examination under 10+2 system of education		2003
12.	Data Entry Operator	6 months	10th Class Passed Typing speed of 30 w.p.m in English/Hindi/Any Local Language.	2012	2003
13.	Dental Laboratory Technician	2 years	Passed 10th class examination under 10+2 system of education.		2003
14.	Desktop Publishing Operator	1 year	Passed 10th class examination under 10+2 system of education	2012	2003
15.	Digital Photographer	1 year	Passed 12th class under 10+2 system of education or equivalent.		2003
16.	Domestic Housekeeping	6 months	Passed 10th class examination under 10+2 System of Education		2003
17.	Dress Making	1 year	Passed Matriculation examination or its equivalent or 10th class under 10 + 2 system.		
18.	Driver Cum Mechanic (Light Motor Vehicle)	6 months	Passed 10th class examination under 10+2 system of education.		2003
19.	Embroidery and Needle work	1 year	Passed 8th class or its equivalent.	2000	
20.	Event Management Assistant	6 months	Passed 10th class examination under 10+2 system of education or its equivalent (with English as a subject).		2003
21.	Fashion Technology	1 year	Passed 12th class under 10+2 system of education or equivalent.		2003
22.	Floriculture and Landscaping	1 year	Passed 10th class examination	2012	2003
23.	Front Office Assistant	6 months	Passed 10+2 class examination under 10+2 system of education or its equivalent (with English as a subject).		2003
24.	Hair and Skin care	1 year	Passed Matriculation examination or equivalent.	1997	
25.	Health Sanitary Inspector	1 year	Passed 12th class examination under 10+2 system of education with science in Class 10. Preference given to trainees with Physics, Chemistry and Biology in 12th Class.		2003

(*Contd.*)

S. No.	Name of the Trade	Duration	Entry Qualification	Syllabus Revised During the Year	Trade Introduced During the Year
26.	Horticulture	1 year	Passed 10th class examination	2012	2003
27.	Hospital Housekeeping	1 year	Passed 12th class examination under 10+2 system of Education with Physics, Chemistry and Biology.		2003
28.	Hospital Waste Management	6 months	Passed 12th class examination under 10+2 system of education with Physics, Chemistry and Biology.		2003
29.	Institution Housekeeping	6 months	Passed 10th class examination under 10+2 system of education.		2003
30.	Insurance Agent	6 months	Passed 12th class under 10+2 system of education or equivalent.		2003
31.	Leather Goods Maker	1 Year	Passed 8th class examination under 10+2 system of education or two classes below matriculation examination or its equivalent.	2008	
32.	Library and Information Science	6 months	Passed 12th class under 10+2 system of education or equivalent.		2003
33.	Litho–Offset Machine Minder	1 year	Passed 10th class examination under 10+2 system of education with Science as one of the subjects or its equivalent.		1998
34.	Manufacture of Footwear	1 year	Passed 8th class examination under 10+2 system of education or its equivalent.	2008	
35.	Medical Transcription	6 months	Passed 12th class examination under 10+2 system of education with Biology/Physiology as major subject. Knowledge of English Language is essential.		2003
36.	Network Technician	6 months	10th Class passed	2012	2003
37.	Old Age Care	6 months	Passed 8th class under 10+2 system of education.		2003
38.	Photographer	1 year	Passed 10th class examination with Physics and Chemistry under 10+2 system or its equivalent.		
39.	Plate Maker-cum-Impositer	1 year	Passed 10th class examination under 10+2 system of education with science as one of the subjects or its equivalent.		1998
40.	Pre/Preparatory School Management (Assistant)	6 months	Passed 10th class examination under 10+2 system of education		2003
41	Fruits and Vegetable Processor	1 year	Passed 10th class examination under 10 + 2 system of education with Science or its equivalent.	2000	

(Contd.)

S. No.	Name of the Trade	Duration	Entry Qualification	Syllabus Revised During the Year	Trade Introduced During the Year
42.	Process Cameraman	1 year	Passed 10th class exam under 10+2 system of education with science as one of the subjects or its equivalent.		1998
43.	Secretarial Practice	1 year	12th class pass	1997	
44.	Stenography (English)	1 year	12th class pass	2002	
45.	Stenography (Hindi)	1 year	12th class pass	2008	
46.	Steward	1 year	Passed 10th class examination under 10+2 system of education or its equivalent.	2005	
47.	Tourist Guide	6 months	Passed 12th class under 10+2 system of education or equivalent.		2003
48.	Weaving of Silk and Woolen Fabrics	1 year	Passed 8th class or its equivalent.		
49.	Weaving of Woolen Fabrics	1 year	Passed 8th class or its equivalent.		
50.	Catering and Hospitality Assistant			2009	
51.	Travel and Tour Assistant			2009	
52.	Multimedia Animation and Special Effects	1 year	10th class pass	2010	
53.	Office Assistant cum Computer Operator	1 year	12th class pass	2010	
54.	Spa Therapy	6 months	Passed 12th class examination under 10+2 system of education or its equivalent		2011
55.	Health, Safety and Environment	1 year	Passed 12th class examination under 10+2 system of education or its equivalent		2011
56.	Firemen	6 months	Passed 10th class examination under 10+2 system of education or its equivalent.		2011
57.	Fire Technology and Industrial Safety Management	1 year	Passed 12th class examination under 10+2 system of education or its equivalent		2011
58.	Human Resource Executive	1 year	Passed 10th class examination		2012
59.	Marketing Executive	1 year	Passed 10th class examination		2012
60.	Finance Executive	1 year	Passed 10th class examination		2012
61.	Para Legal Assistant/ Munshi	6 Months	10th Class Passed		2013
62.	Counselling Skills	6 Months	Class X Passed exam (under 10+2 system of education or its equivalent.)		2013

Appendix VIIA

List (as on 20-5-68) of Trades under CTS of the DGE&T in Respect of Which Diploma/Certificate Awarded from Time to Time have been Recognised by Government of India

Non-Engineering Trades

1. Bleaching, Dyeing and Calico Printing
2. Book Binding
3. Cane, Willow and Bamboo Work
4. Cutting and Tailoring
5. Cutting and Tailoring (Men)
6. Cutting and Tailoring (Women)
7. Confectionery and Bakery (Including Preservation of Fruits)
8. Coir Weaving
9. Embroidery and Needle Work
10. Embroidery and Needle Work (Including Salma, Tila and Lamp and Lamp Shade Work)
11. Fret Work and Manufacture of Wooden Toys
12. Carbo Spinning
13. Hand Composing and Proofreading
14. Hand Weaving of Fancy and Furnishing Fabrics
15. Hand Weaving of Niwar, Tapes, Duries and Carpets
16. Hand Weaving of Wollen Fabrics
17. Knitting with Hand Machine
18. Manufacture of Footwear
19. Manufacture of Household Utensils
20. Manufacture of Sports Goods (Leather)
21. Manufacture of Sports Goods (Miscellaneous)
22. Manufacture of Sports Goods (Woods)
23. Manufacture of Suitcases and other Leather Goods
24. Preservation of Fruits and Vegetables and Manufacture of Confectionery
25. Preservation of Fruits and Vegetables
26. Printing Machine Operator
27. Stenography (English)
28. Stenography (Hindi)
29. Signaller (Railways)
30. Weaving of Silk and Woollen Fabrics
31. Wood Turning and Lacquer Work

*32. Wood Carving and Inlaying

---

* Only Diploma in Craftmanship awarded.

Engineering Trades

1. Blacksmith
2. Building Constructor
3. Carpenter
4. Clock and Watch repairer
5. Die Fitter
6. Draughtsman (Civil)
7. Draughtsman (mechanical)
8. Electrician
9. Electroplater
10. Fitter
11. Grinder
12. Lineman and Wireman
13. Mechanic (Dom. Ref)
14. Mechanic (Instrument)
15. Mechanic (I.C. Engines)
16. Mechanic (Motor)
17. Mechanic (Radio)
18. Mechanic (Tractor)
19. Mechanic (Motor Vehicle)
20. Mechanic (Radio and Television)
21. Mechanic (Diesel)
22. Mechanic (General)
23. Machinist
24. Machinist (Grinder)
25. Machinist (Miller)
26. Machinist (Shaper, Slotter and Planer)
27. Moulder
28. Painter and Decorator
29. Pattern Maker
30. Plumber
31. Painter
32. Mechanic (Refrigeration & Air conditioning)
33. Sheet Metal Worker
34. Surveyor
35. Tool Maker
36. Turner
37. Upholstery
38. Welder (Gas & Electric)
39. Wireless Operator
40. Wireman
41. Watch & Clock Maker

Appendix VIII

Progress Card for Craftsmen Training Scheme (For Engineering Trades only)

PROGRESS CARD

(First Year)

Name of Trainee :
ITI
Roll No. :
Trade :
Date of Admission :
Educational Qualification :
Date of Leaving :

Monthly Tests

No. of Monthly Tests	Practical	Theory	Workshop Calculation and Science	Engineering Drawing	Total	Trade Instructor's Initials	Drawing Instructor's Initials	Mathematics Instructor's Initials	GI's Initials	Remarks
Monthly Test I (Aug.)										
Monthly Test II (Sep.)										
Monthly Test III (Oct.)										
Monthly Test IV (Nov.)										
Monthly Test V (Dec.)										
Monthly Test VI (Jan.)										
Monthly Test VII (Feb.)										
Monthly Test VIII (Mar.)										
Monthly Test IX (Apr.)										
Monthly Test X (May)										
Monthly Test XI (June)										
Monthly Test XII (July)										

Quarterly Assessment							Sessional Marks								
No. of Quarters	Attendance During the Quarter			Loss of Training if any	Extra Hours Suggested to Make up the Training	Progress on Loss of Training	No. of Quarters	Practical 100	Theory 20	Workshop Calculation and Science 10	Engineering Drawing 20	Total 150	Conduct	GI's initial	Principal's Initial
	Actual	Possible	%												
II							II								
III							III								
IV							IV								

*General remarks, if any

PROGRESS CARD

(Second Year)

Monthly Tests

No. of Monthly Tests	Practical	Theory	Workshop Calculation and Science	Engineering Drawing	Total	Trade Instructor's Initials	Drawing Instructor's Initials	Mathematics Instructor's Initials	GI's Initials	Remarks
Monthly Test I (Aug.)										
Monthly Test II (Sep.)										
Monthly Test III (Oct.)										
Monthly Test IV (Nov.)										
Monthly Test V (Dec.)										
Monthly Test VI (Jan.)										
Monthly Test VII (Feb.)										
Monthly Test VIII (Mar.)										
Monthly Test IX (Apr.)										
Monthly Test X (May)										
Monthly Test XI (June) Monthly										
Test XII (July)										

Quarterly Assessment							Sessional Marks								
No. of Quarters	Attendance During the Quarter			Loss of Training if any	Extra Hours Suggested to Make up the Training	Progress on Loss of Training	No. of Quarters	Practical 100	Theory 20	Workshop Calculation and Science 10	Engineering Drawing 20	Total 150	Conduct	GI's initial	Principal's Initial
	Actual	Possible	%												
I.							I.								
II							II								
III							III								
IV							IV								

General remarks, if any

Notes:

1. This progress card should be used for engineering trades only.
2. The maximum and minimum marks should be inserted in the related columns by the concerned instructor.
3. The instructor concerned should make the card up-to-date for each trainee.

PROGRESS CARD FOR CRAFTSMEN TRAINING SCHEME

(For Non-Engineering Trades only)

PROGRESS CARD

Name of Trainee :
Roll No. :
Date of Admission :
Date of Leaving :

ITI :
Trade :
Educational Qualification :

Monthly Tests

No. of Monthly Tests	Practical	Theory	Total	Trade Instructor's Initials	Remarks
Monthly Test I (Aug.)					
Monthly Test II (Sep.)					
Monthly Test III (Oct.)					
Monthly Test IV (Nov.)					
Monthly Test V (Dec.)					
Monthly Test VI (Jan.)					
Monthly Test VII (Feb.)					
Monthly Test VIII (Mar.)					
Monthly Test IX (Apr.)					
Monthly Test X (May)					
Monthly Test XI (June) Monthly Test XII (July)					

Quarterly					Sessional Marks								
No. of Quarters	Attendance During the Quarter	Loss of Training If any	Extra hours Suggested to Make Up the Training	Progress on Loss of Training	No. of Quarters	Practical 100	Theory 20	Total 150	W/S Cal. & Science	Engg. Drg.	Conduct	GI's initial	Principal's Initial
	Actual	Possible	%										
I.					I.								
II.					II.								
III.					III.								
IV.					IV.								

*General remarks, if any

Notes:

1. This progress card should be used for non-engineering trades only.
2. The maximum and minimum marks should be inserted in the related columns by the concerned instructor.
3. The instructor concerned should make the card up-to-date for each trainee.

Appendix IX

List of Engineering Trades under the Craftsmen Training Scheme, Indicating Suitability to PWDs as on 01.01.2010

1. Engineering Trades

S. No.	Name of Trade	Duration	Entry Qualification	Trade Suitable for PWDs
1.	Architectural Assistant	1 year	Passed 10th class examination with 40% marks in Mathematics or Secondary Standard under 10+2 system of education or its equivalent.	OH(LL), HH(P)
2.	Attendant Operator (Chemical Plant)	(a) 2 years (b) 6 months	Passed 10th class examination under 10+2 system of education with Physics, Chemistry and Mathematics as one of the subjects or its equivalent; Passed BSc with Physics and Chemistry.	Not suitable
3.	Building Maintenance	6 months	Passed 10th class examination under 10+2 system of education or its equivalent.	HH
4.	Carpenter	1 year	Passed 8th class examination under 10+2 system of education with Science as one of the subjects or its equivalent.	HH, OH (LL)
5.	Draughtsman (Civil)	2 years	Passed 10th class examination under 10+2 system of education with Science and Mathematics or its equivalent.	OH(LL), HH(P)
6.	Draughtsman (Mechanical)	2 years	Passed 10th class examination under 10+2 system of education with Science and Mathematics or its equivalent.	OH(LL), HH(P)
7.	Electrician	2 years	Passed 10th class examination under 10+2 system of education with Science as one of the subjects or its equivalent.	OH, LV, HH
8.	Electronic Mechanic	2 years	Passed Matriculation examination under 10+2 system of education with Science and Mathematics or its equivalent.	OH, HH
9.	Electroplater	2 years	Passed 10th class examination under 10+2 system of education or its equivalent.	OH, LV
10.	Fitter	2 years	Passed 10th class examination under 10+2 system of education or its equivalent.	OH, LV/Blind, HH
11.	Foundryman	1 year	Passed class 8th examination under 10+2 system of education or its equivalent.	HH(P)
12.	Information Technology and Electronics System Maintenance	2 years	*Essential*—Passed 10th class examination under 10+2 system of education with Science. *Desirable*—Passed 12th class with Mathematics and Physics.	OH, LV
13.	Instrument Mechanic	2 years	Passed 10th class examination under 10+2 system of education with Science as one of the subjects or its equivalent.	OH, HH

(*Contd.*)

S. No.	Name of Trade	Duration	Entry Qualification	Trade Suitable for PWDs
14.	Instrument Mechanic (Chemical Plant)	(a) 2 years (b) 6 months	Passed 10th class examination under 10+2 system of education with Physics, Chemistry and Mathematics as one of the subjects or its equivalent; Passed BSc with Physics and Chemistry.	OH
15.	Interior Decoration and Designing	1 year	Passed 10th class examination under 10+2 system of education or its equivalent	OH, HH
16.	Laboratory Assistant (Chemical Plant)	(a) 2 years (b) 6 months	Passed 10th class examination under 10+2 system of education with Physics, Chemistry and Mathematics as one of the subjects or its equivalent; Passed BSc with Physics and Chemistry.	OH, HH
17.	Lift Mechanic	2 years	Passed 10th class examination under 10+2 system of education with Science or its equivalent.	HH(P)
18.	Machinist	2 years	Passed 10th class examination under 10+2 system of education or its equivalent.	OH, LV, HH
19.	Machinist (Grinder)	2 years	Passed 10th class examination under 10+2 system of education or its equivalent.	OH, LV, HH
20.	Maintenance Mechanic (Chemical Plant)	2 years	Passed 10th class examination with Physics, Chemistry and Mathematics under 10+2 system of education or its equivalent.	OH
21.	Marine Fitter	2 years	Passed 10th class examination under 10+2 system of education with 50% marks in Mathematics and Science or its equivalent.	Not suitable
22.	Mason (Building Constructor)	1 year	Passed 8th class examination under 10+2 system of education or its equivalent.	HH
23.	Mechanic (Communication Equipment Maintenance)	1 year	Passed 10th class examination under 10+2 system of education or its equivalent.	OH(LL)
24.	Mechanic (Repair and Maintenance of Heavy Vehicles)	1 year	Passed 10th class examination under 10+2 system of education or its equivalent.	HH(P), OH(OA)
25.	Mechanic (Repair and Maintenance of Light Vehicles)	1 year	Passed 10th class examination under 10+2 system of education or its equivalent.	HH,OH, LP
26.	Mechanic (Repair and Maintenance of Two-Wheelers)	6 months	Passed 10th class examination under 10+2 system of education or its equivalent.	OH, HH(P)
27.	Mechanic (Diesel)	1 year	Passed 10th class examination under 10+2 system of education or its equivalent.	OH, LV, HH
28.	Mechanic (Motor Vehicle)	2 years	Passed 10th class examination under 10+2 system of education with Science as one of the subjects or its equivalent.	OH, HH
29.	Mechanic (Radio and TV)	2 years	Passed 10th class examination under 10+2 system of education with Science as one of the subjects or its equivalent.	OH
30.	Mechanic (Refrigeration and Air Conditioner)	2 years	Passed 10th class examination under 10+2 system of education with Science and Mathematics or its equivalent.	OH, LV

(*Contd.*)

S. No.	Name of Trade	Duration	Entry Qualification	Trade Suitable for PWDs
31.	Mechanic (Tractor)	1 year	*Essential*—Passed 8th class examination under 10+2 system of education or its equivalent. *Desirable*—Passed 10th class examination under 10+2 system of education with Science (Physics and Chemistry) as one of the subjects or its equivalent.	OH, LV, HH
32.	Mechanic (Agricultural Machinery)	2 years	*Essential*—Passed 8th class examination under 10+2 system of education or its equivalent. *Desirable*—Passed 10th class examination under 10+2 system of education with Science (Physics and Chemistry) as one of the subjects.	OH, LV
33.	Mechanic (Auto Electrical and Electronics)	6 months	Passed 10th class examination under 10+2 system of education with Science and Mathematics or its equivalent.	OH(LL), HH(P)
34.	Mechanic (Computer Hardware)	2 years	Passed 10+2 or Intermediate or Pre-university with Physics as one of the subjects.	OH, HH
35.	Mechanic (Consumer Electronics)	2 years	Passed 10th class examination under 10+2 system of education with Mathematics and Science or its equivalent.	OH, HH
36.	Mechanic (Industrial Electronics)	2 years	Passed 12th class examination with Physics, Chemistry and Mathematics.	OH, HH
37.	Mechanic (Lens/Prism Grinding)	1 year	Passed 10th class examination under 10+2 system of education or its equivalent.	OH, HH
38.	Mechanic (Machine Tools Maintenance)	3 years	Matriculation with Science and Mathematics or its equivalent.	OH
39.	Mechanic (Mechatronics)	2 years	Passed 10+2 class examination with Physics, Chemistry and Mathematics.	OH(LL)
40.	Mechanic (Medical Electronics)	2 years	Passed 10th class examination under 10+2 system of education with Mathematics and Science or its equivalent.	OH(LL), HH(P)
41.	Mechanic-cum-Operator (Electronics Communication System)	2 years	Passed 10th class examination under 10+2 system of education with Science as one of the subjects or its equivalent.	OH(LL)
42.	Operator (Advanced Machine Tools)	2 years	Passed 12th class examination with Physics, Chemistry and Mathematics.	OH(LL), HH(P)
43.	Painter (General)	2 years	Passed 8th class examination or its equivalent.	OH, HH
44.	Physiotherapy Technician	1 year	Passed 12th class examination under 10+2 system of education or its equivalent with Physics, Chemistry and Biology.	OH, HH, LV
45.	Plastic Processing Operator	1 year	Passed 10th class examination under 10+2 system of education or its equivalent.	OH, HH, LV
46.	Plumber	1 year	Passed 8th class examination under 10+2 system of education or its equivalent.	OH, HH, LV
47.	Pump Operator-cum-Mechanic	1 year	Passed 10th class examination under 10+2 system of education with Science or its equivalent.	OH, HH, LV

(Contd.)

S. No.	Name of Trade	Duration	Entry Qualification	Trade Suitable for PWDs
48.	Radiology Technician (Radio Diagnosis and Radiotherapy)	2 years	Passed 12th class examination under 10+2 system of education or its equivalent with Physics, Chemistry and Biology.	Not suitable
49.	Sanitary Hardware Fitter	6 months	Passed 8th class examination under 10+2 system of education or its equivalent.	OH, HH, LV
50.	Sheet Metal Worker	1 year	Passed 8th class examination under 10+2 system of education or its equivalent.	OH, HH, LV
51.	Spinning Technician	2 years	Passed 10th class examination under 10+2 system of education or its equivalent.	OH, HH
52.	Surveyor	2 years	Passed 10th class examination under 10+2 system of education with Science and Mathematics or its equivalent.	OH(OA), HH
53.	Textile Mechatronics	2 years	Passed 10th class examination under 10+2 system of education or its equivalent.	OH(LL), HH(P)
54.	Tool and Die Maker (Dies and Moulds)	3 years	Passed 10th class examination under 10+2 system of education with Science or its equivalent.	OH
55.	Tool and Die Maker (Press Tools, Jigs and Fixtures)	3 years	Passed 10th class examination under 10+2 system of education with Science or its equivalent.	OH
56.	Turner	2 years	Passed 10th class examination under 10+2 system of education or its equivalent.	OH, HH, LV
57.	Vessel Navigator	2 years	Passed 10th class examination under 10+2 system of education with 50% marks in Mathematics and Science or its equivalent.	Not suitable
58.	Welder (Gas and Electric)	1 year	Passed 8th class examination under 10+2 system of education or its equivalent.	OH, HH
59.	Weaving Technician	2 years	Passed 10th class examination under 10+2 system of education with Mathematics and Science or its equivalent.	OH, HH
60.	Wireman	2 years	Passed 8th class examination or its equivalent.	OH, HH, LV
61.	Marine Engine Fitter	1 year	Passed 10th class examination under 10+2 system of education or its equivalent with Mathematics and Science.	

2. Non-Engineering Trades

S. No.	Name of Trade	Duration	Entry Qualification	Trade Suitable for PWDs
1.	Baker and Confectioner	1 year	Passed 10th class examination under 10 + 2 system of education or its equivalent.	OH, HH, LV
2.	Textile (Wet Processing Technician)	2 years	Passed 10th class examination under 10+2 system of education with Science and Mathematics or its equivalent.	OH(LL), HH, LV
3.	Cabin/Room Attendant	6 months	i) Passed 10th class examination under 10+2 system of education. ii) Working knowledge of English and Hindi.	Not suitable

(Contd.)

S. No.	Name of Trade	Duration	Entry Qualification	Trade Suitable for PWDs
4.	Cane Willow and Bamboo Work	1 year	Passed 8th class or its equivalent.	OH, HH, LV
5.	Computer Aided Embroidery and Needlework	6 months	Passed 10th class examination under 10+2 system of education or its equivalent.	OH, HH
6.	Computer Operator and Programming Assistant	1 year	12th class pass under 10+2 system or duly recognized Diploma in Engineering from any polytechnic of 3-year duration after 10th class.	OH, HH, LV
7.	Corporate Housekeeping	6 months	Passed 10th class examination under 10+2 system of education or its equivalent.	OH, HH, LV
8.	Craftsman Food Production (General)	1 year	Passed 10th class examination under 10+2 system of education or its equivalent.	OH, HH
9.	Craftsman Food Production (Vegetarian)	1 year	Passed 10th class examination under 10+2 system of education or its equivalent.	OH, HH
10.	Crèche Management	6 months	Passed 10th class examination under 10+2 system of education or its equivalent.	OH
11.	Cutting and Sewing	1 year	Passed 8th class or its equivalent.	OH, HH, LV
12.	Dairying	1 year	Passed 10th class examination under 10+2 system of education or its equivalent.	OH, HH
13.	Data Entry Operator	6 months	*Essential*—10th class pass (2) Typing speed of 30 wpm in English. *Desirable*—Typing speed of 30 wpm in Hindi/ any local language.	OH, HH, LV
14.	Dental Laboratory Technician	2 years	Passed 10th class examination under 10+2 system of education or its equivalent.	Not suitable
15.	Desktop Publishing Operator	1 year	*Essential*—Passed 12th under 10+2 system or its equivalent; Typing speed of 30 wpm in English. *Desirable*—Typing speed of 30 wpm in any regional language.	OH, HH
16.	Digital Photographer	1 year	Passed 12th class examination under 10+2 system of education or its equivalent.	OH, HH
17.	Domestic Housekeeping	6 months	Passed 10th class examination under 10+2 system of education or its equivalent.	OH, HH, VH
18.	Dressmaking	1 year	Passed Matriculation examination or its equivalent or 10th class under 10+2 system or its equivalent.	OH, HH
19.	Driver Cum Mechanic (Light Motor Vehicle)	6 months	Passed 10th class examination under 10+2 system of education or its equivalent.	Not suitable
20.	Embroidery and Needlework	1 year	Passed 8th class or its equivalent.	OH, HH, LV
21.	Event Management Assistant	6 months	Passed 10th class examination under 10+2 system of education or its equivalent (with English as a subject).	Not suitable
22.	Fashion Technology	1 year	Passed 12th class examination under 10+2 system of education or its equivalent.	OH, HH

(*Contd.*)

S. No.	Name of Trade	Duration	Entry Qualification	Trade Suitable for PWDs
23.	Floriculture and Land-scaping	6 months	Passed 12th class examination under 10+2 system of education or its equivalent Biology as major subject or Vocational Training in Agro-Horticulture.	OH, HH
24.	Front Office Assistant	6 months	Passed 10+2 class examination under 10+2 system of education or its equivalent (with English as a subject).	OH, LV
25.	Hair and Skin Care	1 year	Passed Matriculation examination or equivalent.	OH(LL), HH(P)
26.	Health Sanitary Inspector	1 year	Passed 12th class examination under 10+2 system of education or its equivalent with Science in Class 10; Preference given to trainees with Physics, Chemistry and Biology in 12th Class.	OH(OA)
27.	Horticulture	1 year	Passed 12th class examination under 10+2 system of education or its equivalent with Biology as major subject or Vocational Training in Agro-Horticulture.	OH(OA), HH
28.	Hospital Housekeeping	1 year	Passed 12th class examination under 10+2 system of education or its equivalent with Physics, Chemistry and Biology.	OH, HH, LV
29.	Hospital Waste Management	6 months	Passed 12th class examination under 10+2 system of education or its equivalent with Physics, Chemistry and Biology.	HH
30.	Institution Housekeeping	6 months	Passed 10th class examination under 10+2 system of education or its equivalent.	OH(OA)
31.	Insurance Agent	6 months	Passed 12th class examination under 10+2 system of education or its equivalent.	OH(OA)
32.	Leather Goods Maker	1 year	Passed 8th class examination under 10+2 system of education or two classes below matriculation examination or its equivalent.	OH, HH
33.	Library and Information Science	6 months	Passed 12th class examination under 10+2 system of education or its equivalent.	OH, HH(P), LV
34.	Litho-Offset Machine Minder	1 year	Passed 10th class examination under 10+2 system of education or its equivalent with Science as one of the subjects or its equivalent.	OH, LV
35.	Manufacture of Footwear	1 year	Passed 8th class examination under 10+2 system of education or its equivalent.	OH, HH
36.	Medical Transcription	6 months	Passed 12th class examination under 10+2 system of education or its equivalent with Biology/Physiology as major subjects; Knowledge of English is essential.	OH(LL)
37.	Network Technician	6 months	Passed 12th class examination under 10+2 system of education or its equivalent.	OH(LL), HH(P)
38.	Old-Age Care	6 months	Passed 8th class examination under 10+2 system of education or its equivalent.	Not suitable
39.	Photographer	1 year	Passed 10th class examination with Physics and Chemistry under 10+2 system or its equivalent.	HH
40.	Plate Maker-cum-Impositer	1 year	Passed 10th class examination under 10+2 system of education with Science as one of the subjects or its equivalent.	OH

(*Contd.*)

S. No.	Name of Trade	Duration	Entry Qualification	Trade Suitable for PWDs
41.	Pre/Preparatory School Management (Assistant)	6 months	Passed 10th class examination under 10+2 system of education or its equivalent.	OH(OA)
42.	Preservation of Fruits and Vegetables	1 year	Passed 10th class examination under 10 + 2 system of education with Science or its equivalent.	LV, HH
43.	Process Cameraman	1 year	Passed 10th class examination under 10+2 system of education with Science as one of the subjects or its equivalent.	OH
44.	Secretarial Practice	1 year	Passed 12th class examination under 10+2 system of education or its equivalent.	OH, LV/Blind
45.	Stenography (English)	1 year	Passed 12th class examination under 10+2 system of education or its equivalent.	OH, LV/Blind
46.	Stenography (Hindi)	1 year	Passed 12th class examination under 10+2 system of education or its equivalent.	OH, LV/Blind
47.	Steward	1 year	Passed 10th class examination under 10+2 system of education or its equivalent.	LV
48.	Tourist Guide	6 months	Passed 12th class examination under 10+2 system of education or its equivalent.	OH(OA)
49.	Weaving of Silk and Woolen Fabrics	1 year	Passed 8th class or its equivalent.	LV/Blind, HH
50.	Weaving of Woolen Fabrics	1 year	Passed 8th class or its equivalent.	OH, LV/Blind, HH
51.	Travel and Tour Assistant	1 year	Passed 12th class examination under 10+2 system of education or its equivalent.	OH(OA), LV
52.	Catering and Hospitality Assistant	1 year	Passed 10th class examination under 10+2 system of education or its equivalent.	HH(P)
53.	Multimedia, Animation and Special Effects	1 year	Passed 10th class examination under 10+2 system of education or its equivalent.	OH(LL)
54.	Office Assistant and Computer Operator	1 year	Passed 12th class examination under 10+2 system of education or its equivalent.	OH, HH, LV

Appendix X

Proforma of Record Card of Ex-Trainees Follow-up

1. Name in Full (Block Letters):
2. Father's Name:
3. Full Postal Address:
4. Temporary Address(if different from above):
5. Date and Year of Birth:
6. Physical Fitness:
7. Trade and Year of Passing:
8. Assessment in the Institute:
9. Date of Completion of Training:
10. National Trade Certificate Issued on:
11. Pay Drawn and Scale of Pay, if Employed:
12. If Unemployed and Registered at an Employment Exchange
    (a) Name of the Exchange:
    (b) Registration Number:
    (c) Date of Registration:
13. Particulars of Further Career

Appendix XI

Licenses for Mechanic (Motor Vehicle) Trainees

[To be published in Extraordinary Issue of the Gazette of India, Part II, Section 3, Subsection (i)]

GOVERNMENT OF INDIA
MINISTRY OF SURFACE TRANSPORT
(TRANSPORT WING)

New Delhi, 30th September, 1992

GSR 791 (E) Whereas the Draft of the Driving License (Conditions for Exemption) Rules, 1992, in exercise of the powers conferred by Subsection (2) of Section 3 of the Motor Vehicles Act, 1988 (59 of 1988), was published vide notification No. 676 (E) dated 13th July, 1992 is required by Subsection (1), of Section 212 of the Motor Vehicles Act,1988 (59 of 1988) in the Gazette of India, Extraordinary, Part II, Section 3, Subsection (I) inviting objections and suggestions from all persons likely to be affected thereby within 30 days from the date on which the copies of the said notification is published in the Gazette of India were made available to the public.

And whereas, copies of the said notification were made available to the public on 17th August, 1992. And whereas, no objection and suggestions have been received on the said draft.

Now, therefore, in exercise of the powers conferred by Section 3 (2) of the Motor Vehicles Act, 1988, Central Government hereby makes the following rules, namely:

Rules

1. Short Title and Commencement These rules may be called the Driving License (Conditions for Exemption) Rules, 1992

2. Conditions for Grant of Exemption A person receiving instructions in driving a motor vehicle shall be exempted during training, from the provisions of Subsection (1) of Section 3 of the Motor Vehicles Act, 1988 (59 of 1988) subject to the following conditions, that

(a) Such a person is a trainee undergoing training in an Industrial Training Institute approved by the Central or State Government and driving a light motor vehicle with a written permission of the head of an Industrial Training Institute
(b) Such a person is driving a motor vehicle under the supervision of a duly appointed instructor holding a valid driving licence
(c) Such a person shall not give any vehicle other than a light motor vehicle of the Industrial Training Institute, specially acquired for such training purposes
(d) Such a person is medically fit to drive
(e) The speed of the vehicle shall not exceed 15 km per hour during the training
(f) The training shall be imparted only between 10 a.m. to 5 p.m.
(g) The training shall be imparted only on a light motor vehicle

Sd/-
(G K Pillai)
Joint Secretary to the Government of India
File No. RT – 11036/16/91 – MVL

To,
The Manager
Government of India Press
Mayapuri, New Delhi

Copy to the Transport Secretaries of all the State Governments/Union Territory Administrations

Sd/-
(J R Kapoor)
Desk Officer (MVL)

Appendix XII

Guidelines for Implementation of Specialized Modules for Reorganization of Certificate by National Council for Vocational Training

- The curricula of specialized modules be developed by the respective State Government Association as per the need of the industry and forwarded to DGE&T for record. This curricula would be made available on DGE&T website for use of all State Governments
- The State Government would identify the Industry/industry association and the list may be provided to DG&T. The above list would be approved by Secretary (L&E) and would be posted on the website of DGE&T.
- The State Government along with Industry/Industry association would organize training of six months in industry. Testing and Certification would be done jointly by State Government and Industry .The list of passedout trainees would be maintained by respective State Governments.
- A uniform marking scheme and certificates approved by NCVT would be given to all trainees of Specialized modules. The approved certificate would be made available at the DGE&T website and State Governments can make necessary copies at their end.
- From time to time during training of specialized module, DGE&T would monitor/inspect the quality of training and issue of certificate by deputing senior officers.
- List of successful trainees of specialized modules will be made available at website of respective State Governments under intimation to DGE&T.

Sl. No.

CERTIFICATE

This is to certify that Sh./Km./Smt. ....Son/Daughter/Wife of Shri...has successfully completed six months Training Course in Specialized module " name of the module " in the ....sector at (name of the industry) from ....to.........................and passed the prescribed Trade Test held in __________________________two thousand __________.

Secretary **Authorized Signature & Seal of Industry Partner**

State Council for Vocational Training

PS:

1. This certificate has the recognition of National Council for Vocational Training vide letter No. DGE&T 19(2)/2007-CD, dated 27.6.2008.
2. Prerequisite qualifications for this certificate are National Trade Certificate/National Trade Certificate of Broad Based Basic Training in ....Sector and National Trade Certificate of Advanced Module in ....of..........Sector.

On reverse side

Father's Name:

Date of Birth as recorded in School Certificate:

Appendix XIII

Status of Multi-skill Courses under CTS being implemented through 100 ITIs upgraded to CoE as on 01.01.2007

Sl. No.	Name of the sector	Name of BBBT Modules (one-year duration)	Name of Advanced Modules approved by NCVT (6-month duration)	Name of Advanced modules under ATS
1.	Production and Manufacturing	1. Basic Fitting and Measurement 2. Basic Sheet Metal Worker and Welding 3. Basic Electrical and Electronics and Computer Skill 4. Basic Turning and Grinding 5. Basic Milling and Gear Cutting 6. Basic NC Programming and Operation	1. CNC Machining 2. CAD/CAM 3. PLC and Automation, 4. Quality Engineering, 5. Manufacturing of Jigs and Fixtures 6. Advanced Welding 7. Tool and Die Maker (Dies and Moulds	
2.	Electrical	1. Basic Engineering Skill 2. Basic Electrical Engineering 3. Basic Electronics 4. Basic Electrical Wiring and Winding 5. Basic Power Generation, Transmission and Distribution 6. Basic Computer Operating Skill and its Application	1. Repair and Maintenance of Domestic Appliances. 2. Repair and Maintenance of Instruments used in Electrical Engineering 3. Operation and Maintenance of Equipments used in HT, LT, Substation and Cable Jointing 4. Repair and Maintenance of Electrical Machine and Power Supply 5. Non-Conventional Power Generation, Battery and Inverter	
3.	Electronics	1. Basic Fitting and Soldering 2. Basic Electrical and Electronics 3. Basic Analog Electronics 4. Basic Digital Electronics 5. Basic Measuring Instruments and 6. Basic Computers	1. Radio, Audio, Video System and Appliances 2. Inverters, UPS, Voltage Stabilizers and Industrial Drives 3. Repair and Maintenance of Electronic Test Equipment 4. Communication System, Embedded System and PLC	
4.	Automobile	1. Basic Fitting and Measurement 2. Basic Sheet Metal and Welding 3. Basic Electrical Electronics 4. Basic Microprocessor and Computer Operation 5. Basics of Petrol and Diesel Engine 6. Basics of Transmission, Suspension, Steering System and Brakes	1. Servicing and Overhauling of Automobiles (Petrol) 2. Servicing and Overhauling of Automobiles (Diesel) 3. Auto Electrical Electronics and Air Conditioning in Automobiles 4. Overhauling of Fuel Injection System and Steering Mechanism 5. Denting/Painting and Welding 6. Repair and Maintenance of Wheel; Retrading of Tyres and Wheel Balancing	

(*Contd.*)

Sl. No.	Name of the sector	Name of BBBT Modules (one-year duration)	Name of Advanced Modules approved by NCVT (6-month duration)	Name of Advanced modules under ATS
5.	IT Sector	1. Basic Electrical and Electronics 2. Basic Assembling and Maintenance of PCs 3. Basic Computer Networking 4. Basic Office Automation 5. Basic Internet and Multimedia 6. Basic Database Processing	1. Multimedia and Animation 2. Repair and Maintenance of Hardware of Computer and Peripheral 3. Computer Networking 4. Digital Videography 5. E-Accountancy and Office Management 6. MultiMedia and Creative Designing 7. Information System Management	
6.	Hospitality Sector	1. Basic Food Production 2. Basic Food and Beverages Service (Steward) 3. Basic Front Office Service Operation 4. Basic accommodation operation/ Housekeeping 5. Basic Computer Application 6. Basic Hotel Maintenance	1. Food Production 2. Front Office 3. Food and Beverage Service 4. Housekeeping	
7.	Plastic Processing	1. Basic Fitting and Measurement 2. Basic Electrical and Electronics and Computer Skills 3. Injection Moulding 4. Compression Moulding 5. Extrusion Moulding 6. Blow Moulding	1. Injection Moulding Process 2. Blow Moulding Process, 3. Extrusion Process, and Compression Moulding 4. Ancillary Process	
8.	Refrigeration and Air Conditioning	1. Basic Workshop practices 2. Electrical, Electronic and Electro-Mechanical 3. Basic Refrigeration I 4. Basic Refrigeration II 5. Basic Refrigeration III 6. Basic Refrigeration IV	1. Domestic , Commercial Refrigeration and Air Conditioning 2. Central Air Conditioning Plant, Industrial Cooling and Package 3. Cold Storage, Ice Plant and Ice-Candy Plant	
9.	Instrumentation	1. Basic Engineering Skill-1 2. Basic Engineering Skill-II 3. Basic Electricity and Electrical Instrumentaion 4. Basic Electronics and Electronics instrumentation 5. Basic Measurement and Measuring Instruments 6. Basic Computer Skill	1. Industrial Electronics and Instrumentation 2. Analytical Instrumentation 3. Process Control Instrumentation 4. Medical Instrumentation 5. Optical Instrumentation 6. Electronic Test and Measuring Instruments	

(Contd.)

Sl. No.	Name of the sector	Name of BBBT Modules (one-year duration)	Name of Advanced Modules approved by NCVT (6-month duration)	Name of Advanced modules under ATS
10.	Leather Goods and Footwear	1. Introduction to Leather and Production Knowledge 2. Footwear Technology 3. Footwear Designing 4. Leather Goods Designing and Manufacturing 5. Leather Garments Manufacturing 6. Basic Computer Skills and CAD	1. General ShoeMaking 2. Sports-ShoeMaking and Sports Goods Making 3. Leather Garments Making 4. Travel Goods/ Upholstery/Domestic Item Making	
11.	Chemical	1. Fundamentals of Electronics and Computer 2. Basic Fitting and Measurements 3. Basic Mechanical Processes 4. Fundamental of General Chemistry and Physics 5. Basic Instrumentation 6. Basic Unit Operations and Processes	1. Attendant Operator 2. Maintenance Mechanic 3. Instrument Mechanic 4. Lab Assistant	
12.	Apparel	1. Garment Technology 2. Garment Sewing (Basic Sewing) 3. Garment Sewing (Advanced Sewing) 4. Pattern Making 5. Computerized Pattern Making 6. Quality Control, Finishing and Packing	1. Computer Aided Pattern Making 2. Fashion Designing 3. Shirts and Trousers	
13.	Fabrication	1. Basic Fitting and Measurement 2. Basic Sheet Metal Work and Fastening 3. Basic Machine Shop Practice (turning,milling and grinding). 4. Basic Welding 5. Metals and Surface Finishing Techniques 6. Basic Electrical Electronics and Computer Skills	1. Tig/Mig Welding 2. Structural/Pressure Parts Fitting 3. Structural Welding, 4. Pressure Vessel and Pipe Welding 5. Welding Inspection and Testing	
14.	Construction and Wood Working	1. Basic Architecture 2. Basic Building Construction 3. Basic Carpentry 4. Basic Plumbing 5. Basic Electrical 6. Basic Quality Surveying	1. Concrete Technology 2. Modern Construction Techniques and Management 3. Wood Work in Construction 4. Form Work and Bar Bending	
15.	Food Processing	1. Food Preservation 2. Bakery and Confectionary 3. Milk and Dairy Product 4. Agro Processing 5. Food Beverages 6. Processed Food	1. Food and VegetablesProcessing 2. Cereal, Pulses and Oilseed Processing 3. Food Beverage 4. Milk and Milk Products 5. Meat, Fish and Poultry Processing	

(*Contd.*)

Sl. No.	Name of the sector	Name of BBBT Modules (one-year duration)	Name of Advanced Modules approved by NCVT (6-month duration)	Name of Advanced modules under ATS
16.	Agriculture Machinery	1. Basic Workshop Skill 2. Electrical Wiring and Electronics 3. Tractor and Power Tillers 4. Irrigation Machinery 5. Crop production Machinery 6. Post-Harvest Technology	1. Repair and Maintenance of Harvesting Machines 2. Repair, Maintenance and Overhauling of Tractors 3. Repair, Maintenance of Post-Harvesting Machines/Processing Machines 4. Operation Repair and Maintenance of Crop production Machinery.	
17.	Process Plant Maintenance	1. Basic Fitting 2. Basic Turning and Machining 3. Basic Refrigeration and Air Conditioning 4. Basic Instrumentation 5. Basic Electrician, Electronic and Computer 6. Basic Laboratory Technique	1. Operator Chemical Plant 2. Operation and Maintenance of Boiler and Steam Turbine 3. Mechanical Maintenance of Process Plant 4. Process Plant Mechanical Maintenance 5. Repairing of Equipment 6. Process Plant Refrigeration and Air-Conditioning Maintenance 7. Electrical Maintenance of Process Plant 8. Electronic and Instrument Maintenance of Process Plant 9. Fabrication and Designing of Steel Structure	
18.	Bamboo Technology	1. Basic Electrical and Basic Computer, AutoCAD 2. Basic Course on Bamboo processing 3. Basic Course on Bamboo Processing Machine 4. Basic Course on Secondary Processing of Bamboo 5. Basic Course on Construction and Furniture Making 6. Basic Course on Design Interpretation and Bamboo Handicrafts products	Under preparation	
19.	Tourism	1. Tourism: Concept and Impact 2. Tourism Product of India 3. Geography for Tourism 4. Indian Society, Culture and History 5. Computer Application and Tourism Industry 6. English	1. Eco-Tourism 2. Tour and Travel Management 3. Hospitality Management	

(Contd.)

Sl. No.	Name of the sector	Name of BBBT Modules (one-year duration)	Name of Advanced Modules approved by NCVT (6-month duration)	Name of Advanced modules under ATS
20.	Industrial Automation	1. Workshop Practice 2. Computer Application in Industrial Automation 3. Electronics for Automation 4. Electrical for Automation 5. Process Instrumentation 6. Pneumatics and Hydraulics	1. Industrial Mechanical Maintenance 2. Industrial Electrical Maintenance 3. Industrial Electronics and Control	
21.	Textile Processing and Technology Sector	1. Basic Workshop Practices Fitting and Measurements 2. Basic Electrical, Electronics and Computer Operations 3. Basics of Spinning 4. Basics of Weaving 5. Basics of Bleaching and Finishing 6. Chemistry of Dyeing	1. Advanced Spinning and Weaving Technology 2. Advanced Bleaching Finishing and Dying Technology 3. Repair and Maintenance of Textile Machinery and Equipment 4. Advanced Textile Technology 5. Technology of Sizing, Bleaching and Finishing 6. Technology of Dyeing 7. Technology of Printing 8. Computer Aided Textile, Design and Colour 9. Testing of Chemicals and Textiles	
22.	Rubber Technology Sector	1. Synthetic Rubber & Reclaimed Rubber 2. Rubber Compounding and Vulcanization 3. Manufacture of Latex Products 4. Manufacture of Dry Rubber products 5. Design, Development and Testing of Rubber products 6. Basic Electrical & Basic Computer, Auto Cad	1. Manufacture of Industrial Rubber products 2. Manufacture of HealthCare products 3. Laboratory Work Testing	

Appendix XIV

Specialised Module Under Apprenticeship Training (as on December 2013)

Group No. 35 – Centre of Excellence Trades Group:

1.	Mechanic Automobile (Advance Petrol Engine)	7233.22	1:2	Two years	Broad Based Basic Training in Automobile Sector under Centre of Excellence Scheme and Advanced module of Centre of Excellence Scheme in Servicing and Overhauling of Automobiles (Petrol).	One year and six months	Passed 10th class examination under 10+2 system of education or its equivalent.
2.	Mechanic Automobile (Advance Diesel Engine)	7233.24	1:2	Two years	Broad Based Basic Training in Automobile Sector under Centre of Excellence Scheme and Advanced module of Centre of Excellence Scheme in Servicing and Overhauling of Automobiles (Diesel).	One year and six months	Passed 10th class examination under 10+2 system of education or its equivalent.
3.	Mechanic Auto Electronics	7242.10	1:2	Two years	Broad Based Basic Training in Automobile Sector under Centre of Excellence Scheme and Advanced module of Centre of Excellence Scheme in Auto Electrical, Auto Electronics and Air-conditioning in Automobiles.	One year and six months	Passed 10th class examination under 10+2 system of education or its equivalent.
4.	Mechanic (Denting, Painting and Welding)	7142.20 7213.30	1:2	Two years	Broad Based Basic Training in Automobile Sector under Centre of Excellence Scheme and Advanced module of Centre of Excellence Scheme in Denting(Painting and Welding).	One year and six months	Passed 10th class examination under 10+2 system of education or its equivalent.
5.	TIG/MIG Welder	7212.10 7212.20 7212.30 7212.65 8231.35	1:3	Two years	Broad Based Basic Training in Fabrication (Fitting & Welding) Sector under Centre of Excellence Scheme and Advanced module of Centre of Excellence Scheme in TIG/MIG Welding.	One year and six months	Passed 10th class examination under 10+2 system of education or its equivalent.
6.	Structural Welder	7212.10 7212.20 7212.30 7212.65 8231.35	1:3	Two years	Broad Based Basic Training in Fabrication (Fitting & Welding) Sector under Centre of Excellence Scheme and Advanced module of Centre of Excellence Scheme in Structural Welding.	One year and six months	Passed 10th class examination under 10+2 system of education or its equivalent.
7.	Welder (Pipe and Pressure Vessels)	7212.10 7212.20 7212.30 7212.65 8231.35	1:2	Two years	Broad Based Basic Training in Fabrication (Fitting and Welding) Sector under Centre of Excellence Scheme and Advanced module of Centre of Excellence Scheme in Pressure Vessels and Pipe Welding.	One year and six months	Passed 10th class examination under 10+2 system of education or its equivalent.

(Contd.)

8.	Chemical Laboratory Assistant	3111.30	1:2	Two years	Broad Based Basic Training in Chemical Sector under Centre of Excellence Scheme and Advanced module of Centre of Excellence Scheme in Laboratory Assistant.	One year and six months	Passed 10th class exam. under 10+2 system of education or its equivalent.
9.	Advance Mechanic (Instruments)	7311.10 7311.30 7241.10	1:2	Two years	Broad Based Basic Training in Chemical Sector under Centre of Excellence Scheme and Advanced module of Centre of Excellence Scheme in Instruments Mechanic.	One year and six months	Passed 10th class examination under 10+2 system of education or its equivalent.
10.	CAD-CAM Operator cum Programmer	3121.20	1:2	Two years	Broad Based Basic Training in Production and Manufacturing Sector under Centre of Excellence Scheme and Advanced module of Centre of Excellence Scheme in CAD/ CAM.	One year and six months	Passed 10th class examination under 10+2 system of education or its equivalent.
11.	Advance Welder	7212.10 7212.20 7212.30 7212.65 8231.35	1:2	Two years	Broad Based Basic Training in Production and Manufacturing Sector under Centre of Excellence Scheme and Advanced module of Centre of Excellence Scheme in Advanced Welding.	One year and six months	Passed 10th class examination under 10+2 system of education or its equivalent.
12.	Jigs and Fixtures Maker	7222.30	1:2	Two years	Broad Based Basic Training in Production and Manufacturing Sector under Centre of Excellence Scheme and Advanced module of Centre of Excellence Scheme in Manufacturing of Jigs and Fixtures.	One year and six months	Passed 10th class examination under 10+2 system of education or its equivalent.
13.	Quality Assurance Assistant	3152.90	1:2	Two years	Broad Based Basic Training in Production and Manufacturing Sector under Centre of Excellence Scheme and Advanced module of Centre of Excellence Scheme in Quality Engineering.	One year and six months	Passed 10th class examination under 10+2 system of education or its equivalent.
14.	CNC Programmer cum Operator	3121.20	1: 3	Two years	Broad Based Basic Training in Production and Manufacturing Sector under Centre of Excellence Scheme and Advanced module of Centre of Excellence Scheme in CNC Machining.	One year and six months	Passed 10th class examination under 10+2 system of education or its equivalent.
15.	Operator PLC System	8211.90	1:2	Two years	Broad Based Basic Training in Production and Manufacturing Sector under Centre of Excellence Scheme and Advanced module of Centre of Excellence Scheme in PLC and Automation.	One year and six months	Passed 10th class examination under 10+2 system of education or its equivalent.
16.	Mechanic (Electrical Domestic Appliances)	7233.58	1:2	Two years	Broad Based Basic Training in Electrical Sector under Centre of Excellence Scheme and Advanced module of Centre of Excellence Scheme in Repair and Maintenance of Domestic Appliances.	One year and six months	Passed 10th class examination under 10+2 system of education or its equivalent.

(Contd.)

17.	Mechanic (HT, LT Equipments and Cable Jointing)	7245.20	1:2	Two years	Broad Based Basic Training in Electrical Sector under Centre of Excellence Scheme and Advanced module of Centre of Excellence Scheme in Operation and Maintenance of equipments used in HT, LT Substation and Cable Jointing.	One year and six months	Passed 10th class examination under 10+2 system of education or its equivalent.
18.	Mechanic (Electrical Power Drives)	7241.20 7242.10	1:2	Two years	Broad Based Basic Training in Electrical Sector under Centre of Excellence Scheme and Advanced module of Centre of Excellence Scheme in Repair and Maintenance of Electrical machines and Power Supply.	One year and six months	Passed 10th class examination under 10+2 system of education or its equivalent.
19.	Mechanic (Embedded Systems and PLC)	8211.90	1:2	Two years	Broad Based Basic Training in Electronics Sector under Centre of Excellence Scheme and Advanced module of Centre of Excellence Scheme in Embedded Systems and PLC.	One year and six months	Passed 10th class examination under 10+2 system of education or its equivalent.
20.	Mechanic Power Electronics (Inverters, UPS and Maintenance of Drives)	7241.10 7242.10	1:2	Two years	Broad Based Basic Training in Electronics Sector under Centre of Excellence Scheme and Advanced module of Centre of Excellence Scheme in Inverters, UPS, Voltage Stabilizer and Industrial Drives.	One year and six months	Passed 10th class examination under 10+2 system of education or its equivalent.
21.	Mechanic (DTH and other Communication System)	7243.10 7244.20	1:2	Two years	Broad Based Basic Training in Electronics Sector under Centre of Excellence Scheme and Advanced module of Centre of Excellence Scheme in Communication System.	One year and six months	Passed 10th class examination under 10+2 system of education or its equivalent.
22.	Mechanic (Domestic, Commercial Refrigeration and Air Conditioning Machines)	7233.50	1:2	Two years	Broad Based Basic Training in Refrigeration and Air-conditioning Sector under Centre of Excellence Scheme and Advanced module of Centre of Excellence Scheme in Domestic, Commercial Refrigeration and Air Conditioning.	One year and six months	Passed 10th class examination under 10+2 system of education or its equivalent.
23.	Mechanic (Central Air conditioning Plant, Industrial cooling and Package Air conditioning)	8281.25 8169.30	1:2	Two years	Broad Based Basic Training in Refrigeration and Air-conditioning Sector under Centre of Excellence Scheme and Advanced module of Centre of Excellence Scheme in Central Air conditioning Plant, Industrial cooling and Package Air-conditioning.	One year and six months	Passed 10th class examination under 10+2 system of education or its equivalent.
24.	Mechanic (Cold storage, Ice plant and Ice candy plant)	7413.50 8169.30	1:2	Two years	Broad Based Basic Training in Refrigeration and Air-conditioning Sector under Centre of Excellence Scheme and Advanced module of Centre of Excellence Scheme in Cold storage, Ice plant and Ice candy plant.	One year and six months	Passed 10th class examination under 10+2 system of education or its equivalent.

(Contd.)

25.	Computer Aided Pattern Maker	7222.80 7422.38 7434.20 7435.10 7442.16	1:2	Two years	Broad Based Basic Training in Apparel Sector under Centre of Excellence Scheme and Advanced module of Centre of Excellence Scheme in Computer Aided and Pattern Making.	One year and six months	Passed 10th class examination under 10+2 system of education or its equivalent.
26.	Fashion Designing Assistant	3471.40	1:2	Two years	Broad Based Basic Training in Apparel Sector under Centre of Excellence Scheme and Advanced module of Centre of Excellence Scheme in Fashion Designing.	One year and six months	Passed 10th class examination under 10+2 system of education or its equivalent.
27.	Shirts and Trousers Maker	7433.25 7433.30	1:4	Two years	Broad Based Basic Training in Apparel Sector under Centre of Excellence Scheme and Advanced module of Centre of Excellence Scheme in Shirts and Trousers.	One year and six months	Passed 10th class examination under 10+2 system of education or its equivalent.
28.	Mechanic (Non-conventional Power Generation, Battery and Inverter)	8282.10	1:5	Two years	Broad Based Basic Training in Electrical Sector under Centre of Excellence Scheme and Advanced module of Centre of Excellence Scheme in Non-conventional Power Generation, Battery and Inverter.	One year and six months	Passed 10th class examination under 10+2 system of education or its equivalent.
29.	Mechanic (Repair and Maintenance of instruments used in Electrical Engineering)	7241.10	1:5	Two years	Broad Based Basic Training in Electrical Sector under Centre of Excellence Scheme and Advanced module of Centre of Excellence Scheme in Repair and Maintenance of instruments used in Electrical Engineering.	One year and six months	Passed 10th class examination under 10+2 system of education or its equivalent.
30.	Extrusion Machine Operator (Plastic)	8232.20	1:3	Two years	Broad Based Basic Training in Plastic Processing Sector under Centre of Excellence Scheme and Advanced module of Centre of Excellence Scheme in Extrusion Process.	One year and six months	Passed 10th class examination under 10+2 system of education or its equivalent.
31.	Injection Moulding Machine Operator	8232.25	1:3	Two years	Broad Based Basic Training in Plastic Processing Sector under Centre of Excellence Scheme and Advanced module of Centre of Excellence Scheme in Injection Moulding Process.	One year and six months	Passed 10th class examination under 10+2 system of education or its equivalent.
32.	Blow Moulding Machine Operator	8232.35	1:3	Two years	Broad Based Basic Training in Plastic Processing Sector under Centre of Excellence Scheme and Advanced module of Centre of Excellence Scheme in Blow Moulding Process.	One year and six months	Passed 10th class examination under 10+2 system of education or its equivalent.
33.	House Keeper (Hotel)	5121.10	1:5	Two years	Broad Based Basic Training in Hospitality Sector under Centre of Excellence Scheme and Advanced module of Centre of Excellence Scheme in Accommodation Operation/ House Keeping.	One year and six months	Passed 10th class examination under 10+2 system of education or its equivalent.

(*Contd.*)

34.	Assistant Front Office Manager	5121.25	1:5	Two years	Broad Based Basic Training in Hospitality Sector under Centre of Excellence Scheme and Advanced module of Centre of Excellence Scheme in Front Office Management.	One year and six months	Passed 10th class examination under 10+2 system of education or its equivalent.
35.	Apprentice Food Production (Cookery)	5122.20	1:5	Two years	Broad Based Basic Training in Hospitality Sector under Centre of Excellence Scheme and Advanced module of Centre of Excellence Scheme in Food Production (Cookery).	One year and six months	Passed 10th class examination under 10+2 system of education or its equivalent.
36.	Apprentice Food and Beverage Service (Stewardship)	5123.20	1:5	Two years	Broad Based Basic Training in Hospitality Sector under Centre of Excellence Scheme and Advanced module of Centre of Excellence Scheme in Food and Beverage Service (Stewardship).	One year and six months	Passed 10th class examination under 10+2 system of education or its equivalent.
37.	Computer and Peripherals Hardware Repair and Maintenance Mechanic	3114.10 5220.25	1:4	Two years	Broad Based Basic Training in Information Technology Sector under Centre of Excellence Scheme and Advanced module of Centre of Excellence Scheme in Repair and Maintenance of Hardware of Computer and Peripherals.	One year and six months	Passed 10th class examination under 10+2 system of education or its equivalent.
38.	Computer Networking Technician	4122.10 4112.20 4113.35	1:4	Two years	Broad Based Basic Training in Information Technology Sector under Centre of Excellence Scheme and Advanced module of Centre of Excellence Scheme in Computer Networking.	One year and six months	Passed 10th class examination under 10+2 system of education or its equivalent.
39.	Multimedia and Web Page Designer	4113.30	1:4	Two years	Broad Based Basic Training in Information Technology Sector under Centre of Excellence Scheme and Advanced module of Centre of Excellence Scheme in Multimedia and Web Page Designing.	One year and six months	Passed 10th class examination under 10+2 system of education or its equivalent.
40.	Process Plant Operator	8152.10	1:3	Two years	Broad Based Basic Training in Process Plant Maintenance Sector under Centre of Excellence Scheme and Advanced module of Centre of Excellence Scheme in Operator Chemical Plant.	One year and six months	Passed 10th class examination under 10+2 system of education or its equivalent.
41.	Utility Operator	8161.30	1:3	Two years	Broad Based Basic Training in Process Plant Maintenance Sector under Centre of Excellence Scheme and Advanced module of Centre of Excellence Scheme in Operation and Maintenance of Boiler and Steam Turbine.	One year and six months	Passed 10th class examination under 10+2 system of education or its equivalent.
42.	Maintenance Mechanic	8159.79	1:3	Two years	Broad Based Basic Training in Process Plant Maintenance Sector under Centre of Excellence Scheme and Advanced module of Centre of Excellence Scheme in Mechanical Maintenance of Process Plant.	One year and six months	Passed 10th class examination under 10+2 system of education or its equivalent.

(Contd.)

43.	Electrical Mechanic	7241.20	1:3	Two years	Broad Based Basic Training in Process Plant Maintenance Sector under Centre of Excellence Scheme and Advanced module of Centre of Excellence Scheme in Electrical Maintenance of Process Plant.	One year and six months	Passed 10th class examination under 10+2 system of education or its equivalent.
44.	Instrument Controller	7241.10	1:3	Two years	Broad Based Basic Training in Process Plant Maintenance Sector under Centre of Excellence Scheme and Advanced module of Centre of Excellence Scheme in Electronic and Instrument Maintenance of Process Plant.	One year and six months	Passed 10th class examination under 10+2 system of education or its equivalent.
45.	Technician Fabricator	7212.30	1:3	Two years	Broad Based Basic Training in Process Plant Maintenance Sector under Centre of Excellence Scheme and Advanced module of Centre of Excellence Scheme in Fabrication and Designing of Steel Structure.	One year and six months	Passed 10th class examination under 10+2 system of education or its equivalent.
46	Mechanic Radio, Audio, Video System and Appliances	7243.70 7243.90	1:3	Two years	Broad Based Basic Training in Electronics Sector under Centre of Excellence Scheme and Advanced module of Centre of Excellence Scheme in Radio, Audio, Video System and Appliances	One year and six months	Passed 10th class examination under 10+2 system of education or its equivalent.
47.	Mechanic Repair and Maintenance of Electronics Test Equipment	7243.10	1:3	Two years	Broad Based Basic Training in Electronics Sector under Centre of Excellence Scheme and Advanced module of Centre of Excellence Scheme in Repair and Maintenance of Electronics Test Equipment	One year and six months	Passed 10th class examination under 10+2 system of education or its equivalent.
48.	Mechanic Automobile Electronics	7231.10	1:3	Two years	Broad Based Basic Training in Electronics Sector under Centre of Excellence Scheme and Advanced module of Centre of Excellence Scheme in Automobile Electronics	One year and six months	Passed 10th class examination under 10+2 system of education or its equivalent.
49.	Mechanic Mechanical Maintenance (Industrial Automation)	7233.38	1:3	Two years	Broad Based Basic Training in Industrial Automation Sector under Centre of Excellence Scheme and Advanced module of Centre of Excellence Scheme in Mechanical Maintenance for Automation	One year and six months	Passed 10th class examination under 10+2 system of education or its equivalent.
50.	Mechanic Electrical Maintenance (Industrial Automation)	7241.70	1:3	Two years	Broad Based Basic Training in Industrial Automation Sector under Centre of Excellence Scheme and Advanced module of Centre of Excellence Scheme in Electrical Maintenance for Automation	One year and six months	Passed 10th class examination under 10+2 system of education or its equivalent.
51.	PLC Operator	7233.38	1:3	Two years	Broad Based Basic Training in Industrial Automation Sector under Centre of Excellence Scheme and Advanced module of Centre of Excellence Scheme in Automation and PLC	One year and six months	Passed 10th class examination under 10+2 system of education or its equival

Appendix XIV – A

Proforma for Register of Caution Money Deposits

Sl. No.	Name of the Trade	Roll No. of the Trainee	Name of the Trainee	Father's Name	Receipt No. and Date	Amount	Date of Admission	Date of Completion of Training	Date of Refund of Caution Money of Trainee	Amount Refunded	Dated Signature of the Trainee	Remarks

Monthly Abstract of Caution Money Deposits at the End of Month

Opening Balance		Total	Receipt during the Month	Total	Payments to Trainees	Balance	Signature of Principal
Cash in Hand	Balance in Treasury						

Cash Book of Caution Money for the .... Of .... 19 ....

Receipt							Payments						
Date	No. of Receipt where necessary	Particulars	Folio	Cash ₹ P	Treasury ₹ P	Total ₹ P	Date	No. of Voucher	Particulars	Folio	Cash ₹ P	Treasury ₹ P	Total ₹ P

Appendix XV

Inspection Questionnaire
(For Technical Inspection of Industrial Training Institutes)

GUIDELINES FOR INSPECTION OF INDUSTRIAL TRAINING INSTITUTES

The Directorate General of Employment & Training(DG&T) is responsible for laying down standards, syllabi and general policy for training in the Industrial Training Institutes under the Craftsmen Training Scheme. Final National Trade Certificates are also issued under the signature of Deputy Director General of Training who is ex-officio Secretary, National Council for Vocational Training.

To ensure that the norms and standards laid down by NCVT are followed with letter and spirit in the ITIs, inspections at regular interval are carried out by the officers of DGE&T from time to time.

To facilitate inspection of these institutes, guidelines have been prepared. Inspecting Officers may check the points given in the guidelines while undertaking the inspection. Although they cover all the essential points, yet it cannot be said to be exhaustive. So the Inspecting Officer may use his/her discretion and look into other aspects in the working of the institutes in order to assess the general standard of training.

I. General

(i) Name of the Institute
(ii) Name and designation of the Inspecting officer
(iii) Date of Inspection
(iv) Date on which the last inspection was carried out by the DGE&T
(v) Indicate the name and designation of the officer
(vi) Normal working hours of the institute

2. Procedure Followed For Admission

3. Medical Examination of the Trainees Whether done at the time of admission/during the session.

4. Procedure Followed for Grant of Stipend to the Deserving Trainees, Rate of Stipend

5. Supply of Uniform, Stationery, Etc. to the Trainees

6. Strength of the Institute

S. No.	Trade	Number of Trainees During the Last Three Years								
		Year*			Year*			Year*		
		Admitted	Drop-out	Passed	Admitted	Drop-out	Passed	Admitted	Drop-out	Passed

*Furnish information for the last three years.

7. Position of Staff

Designation	Sanctioned Strength	Present Strength	Shortfall	Remarks

8. Training Standard (Fill up the information as per the proforma at Annexure I of this Appendix for each trade)

9. Machinery and Equipment (Fill up the information as per the proforma at Annexure I of this Appendix for each trade)

10. Building (Space available for classrooms, workshops, office, stores, etc. Whether adequate or not. Information relating to land)

11. Attendance and Discipline

(a) General discipline in the institute
(b) Attendance records, etc. maintained
(c) Steps taken to ensure punctuality

12. Issue of Certificates in Time

(i) Provisional
(ii) Final
(iii) Availability of copies of blank National Trade Certificate

13. General Standard of the Staff

14. Steps Taken for Upgradation of Knowledge and Standard of the Staff How many staff members have been trained in Methods of Instruction(from CTIs, ATIs and CSTARI) and in advanced skills(from ATIs and CTI). Programmes for training those still untrained.

15. Power and Water (Whether available in adequate quantity or not)

16. Stores

(i) Adequacy of space
(ii) Layout
(iii) Arrangement for receipts and issues
(iv) Results of test checks

17. Library

(i) General condition of the Library
(ii) Availability of sufficient number of books, technical magazines, etc.
(iii) Availability of syllabi of the various trades and question papers
(iv) Availability of instructional material as prepared by the DGET (CSTARI, Kolkata; RDAT, Kanpur; and CIMI, Chennai, etc.)
(v) Availability of funds
(vi) Utilization by staff and trainees

18. Amenities for Trainees

(i) Medical facilities, first aid, etc.
(ii) Facilities of toilet, drinking water, etc.
(iii) Facilities of sports, recreation, etc.(whether funds, etc. available)

19. Hostels

(i) Adequacy of rooms available
(ii) General sanitary conditions
(iii) Facilities for extra-curricular activities
(iv) Arrangement for mess

20. Safety

(i) Steps taken for safety of trainees and equipment in the workshops
(ii) Steps taken for prevention of fire

21. Special Facilities, if any given to SC/ST Trainees

22. Number of Women Trainees, Physically Handicapped Trainees—Details Tradewise

23. Follow up action Taken and Employment Position of Passed-out Trainees

24. Advisory Committees; how often they meet

25. Last Inspection carried out by State Directorate

26. Expenditure Incurred on Raw Material Per Month Per Trainee

27. Effective use of instructional materials—whether use is being made of the Publication of CSTARI/RDAT/CIMI

PROFORMA

Name of the Trade :
Number of Units :

1. Strength of Trainees

S. No.	Trade	Number of Trainees During the Last Three Years								
		Year *			Year *			Year *		
		Admitted	Drop-out	Passed	Admitted	Drop-out	Passed	Admitted	Drop-out	Passed

*Furnish information for the last three years.

2. *Staffing Position*

Designation	Sanctioned Strength	Actual Strength	Shortfall	Remarks

3. *General Standard of the Staff*

4. *Machinery and Equipment*

(i) Whether available as per norms of NCVT?
(ii) List the machines which fall short against the prescribed norms.
(iii) Whether machines utilized to their full capacity?
(iv) List the machines which are old and need replacement.
(v) Whether proper maintenance of machines done. System of maintenance followed?

5. *Training Standard*

(i) Availability of latest copies of the syllabi
(ii) Logical break-up of syllabi by the Instructors, in respect of
  (a) Time Schedule
  (b) Lesson Plan
  (c) Demonstration Plan
(iii) Use of Audio-visual Aids in training; Results of test checks
(iv) Preparation and updating of instructional material prepared by the instructors
(v) Design of practical exercises for covering the entire syllabi
(vi) Availability of adequate quantity of raw material for carrying out practical exercises
(vii) Periodic assignment of progress of trainees and system followed for evaluation
(viii) Arrangements for industrial visits for the trainees
(ix) Item of commercial utility manufactured by the trainees
(x) Does the training imparted over various machines in your view enough to meet industrial demand?
(xi) Application of special tools
(xii) Measures taken by the Instructors to uplift the trainees lacking in skills as identified from the evaluation of exercises
(xiii) Any specific problem in skill training

6. *Conclusions and Recommendations* **Note:** While carrying out inspection in a section/trade, frank discussion may be held with the instructors and trainees of the trade regarding the various problems encountered during the process of training and their suggestions for improvement. Result on test checks on instructors and trainees should also be recorded.

Signature
Name of the Inspecting Officer
Designation
Date

Appendix XVI

The Proforma of the Requisite Information regarding Inspection Carried out

STATE ....

Bi-annual Statement of Inspection of Industrial Training Institutes for the half year ended on ....

Sl. No.	Name of ITI	Category of Inspection			
		A	B	C	Total
1	2	3	4	5	6
Total: Inspections carried out for each category:					

Note:

A - Inspection carried out by officers of this Directorate.

B - Inspection carried out by the tripartite team.

C - Inspection carried out by the DGE&T.

Signature of Director

Appendix XVII

TS – 1

Annual Statistical Return on Craftsmen Training Scheme

Name and Address of the Training Institute (Govt./Private) ....

Report of the Session commencing from August (as on 30th September) ....

S. No	Number of seats sanctioned		No. of applications for fresh admission	Number of trainees on roll			Number of				Remarks
	Up to the end of the last session	During the current session		Up to the end of the last session	During the current session	Total	SC included in Col. 7	ST included in Col. 7	Physically Handicapped in Col. 7	Ex-servicemen included in Col. 7	
1	2	3	4	5	6	7	8	9	10	11	12
1. No. of Engg. Trades (Two Years) = ... Nos.											
2. No. of Engg. Trades (One year) = ... Nos.											
3. No. of Non-Engg. Trades = ... Nos.											

Notes:

(i) Figures in respect of women trainees may be given separately for each of the three groups within brackets below overall figures reported under each of Col (2 to 11)

(ii) Category of Institute

For General—G | For Women—W
For SC—SC | For ST—ST
For Physically Handicapped - Ph | For Minority—M

(iii) This Return is to be submitted by ITIs to DGE&T, New Delhi, through the State Director.

Signature : Head of the Institute

Appendix XVIII

TS – 2

Annual Statistical Return Showing Number of Trainees Declared Successful under Craftsmen Training Scheme in Final/Supplementary Trade Tests

1. Name and Address of the Institute (Govt./Private) ....
2. Report for the session ending Month/Year and supplementary exam. held ....
3. Category of the Institute .... During .... Month/Year

Sl. No.	Group	No. of trainees appeared in		No. of trainees passed		Remarks if any
		Final trade test at the end of training	Supplementary trade at the end of training during (......... Month/ Year	Final trade test	Supplementary trade test	
1	2	3	4	5	6	7
1. No. of Engg. Trades (Two Years) = ... Nos. 2. No. of Engg. Trades (One year) = ... Nos. 3. No. of Non-Engg. Trades = ... Nos.						

Notes :

1. Figures in respect of women trainees may be given separately for each of the three groups within brackets below overall figures reported under each of Columns (3 to 6)
2. Category of Trainees

   For General—G
   For Women—W
   For SC—SC
   For ST—ST
   For Physically Handicapped—Ph
   For Minority—M
3. This Return is to be submitted by ITIs to DGE&T, New Delhi, through the State Director.

Signature: Head of the Institute

Appendix XIX

TS – 3
Annual Statistical Return of ITIs under Craftsmen Training Scheme Trades and Units existing and affiliated to NCVT

1. Name and Address of the Institute (Govt./Private) ....
2. Report for session ending on 31st July
3. Category of the Institute

Sl No.	Name of Trades existing at the Institute	Number of Units	Units affiliated to NCVT	Remarks, if any
1	2	3	4	5
A. Engineering Trades				
1.				
2.				
3.				
B. Non-Engineering Trades				
1.				
2.				
3.				

Notes :

1. Figures under columns 3 and 4, number of women units may be shown separately in brackets.
2. Category of trainees

   For General—G　　For Women—W

   For SC—SC　　For ST—ST

   For Physically Handicapped—Ph　　For Minority—M
3. This Return is to be submitted by ITIs to DGE&T, New Delhi, through the State Director.

Signature: Head of the Institute

Appendix XX

TS – 4

Annual Statistical Return relating to training of Industrial Workers under Scheme of Part-time Classes for Industrial Workers.

1. Name and Address of the Institute (Govt./Private) ……………………………
2. Report for the year ending December
3. Category of the Institute

Trade	No. of Seats Introduced	No. of Trainees on roll at the end of year	No. of SC included in Col. 3	No. of ST included in Col. 3	No. of Phy. Handicapped in Col. 3	No. of Ex-Serviceman included in Col.3	No. of workers of Previous Batch Passed out
1	2	3	4	5	6	7	8
Total							

Notes:

1. Figures in respect of women trainees may be given separately for each of the three groups within brackets below overall figures reported under each of Columns (3 to 8)
2. Category of trainees

   For General—G | For Women—W
   For SC—SC | For ST—ST
   For Physically Handicapped—Ph | For Minority—M
3. This Return is to be submitted by ITIs to DGE&T, New Delhi, through the State Director.

Signature : Head of the Institute

Appendix XXI

Sl. ....

Certificate of Merit for the Best Trainee

GOVERNMENT OF INDIA
DIRECTORATE GENERAL OF EMPLOYMENT & TRAINING
MINISTRY OF LABOUR & EMPLOYMENT

This is to certify that Sh./Km./Smt. ....son/daughter/ wife of Shri..................................has undergone a course of training in the trade of ....at the Industrial Training Institute...................during the session.............and was adjudged as the BEST CRAFTSMAN in that trade in India at the All India Competition held in ....

In appreciation of the splendid effort put in by Sh./Km./Smt. ...., he/she is hereby awarded this Certificate of Merit.

New Delhi, the 20

Director General of Employment & Training/
Joint Secretary to the Govt. of India

Appendix XXII

क्र. सं. बी. आई. टी./05
S. No. B.I.T.J./05

No. 000076

भारत सरकार
GOVERNMENT OF INDIA
श्रम एवं रोजगार मंत्रालय
MINISTRY OF LABOUR AND EMPLOYMENT
रोज़गार और प्रशिक्षण महानिदेशालय
Directorate General of Employment and Training

अखिल भारतीय कौशल प्रतियोगिता
ALL INDIA SKILL COMPETITION
शिल्पकार प्रशिक्षण योजना के अन्तर्गत
UNDER CRAFTSMAN TRAINING SCHEME
सर्वोत्तम ओद्योगिक प्रशिक्षण संस्थान/केन्द्र
BEST INDUSTRIAL TRAINING INSTITUTE/CENTRE

श्रेष्ठता प्रमाण–पत्र

CERTIFICATE OF MERIT

प्रमाणित किया जाता है कि .... जिसके प्रशिक्षणार्थियों ने ...., दो हजार .... में हुई अखिल भारतीय कौशल प्रतियोगिता में .... व्यवसाय में अधिकतम अंक प्राप्त किए, को उपर्युक्त व्यवसाय में योजना के अन्तर्गत सर्वोत्तम औद्योगिक प्रशिक्षण संस्थान/केन्द्र निर्णात किया गया। .... व्यवसाय में शिल्पकार प्रशिक्षण देने का सराहनीय कार्य करने के सम्मान में यह दक्षता का प्रमाण–पत्र प्रदान किया जाता है।

This is to certify that .... whose trainee secured the highest total marks in the trade of .... in the All India Skill Competition held in .... two thousand ..... has been adjudged as the Best Industrial Training Institute/Centre under the scheme, in the above trade.

In appreciation of the meritorious effort for imparting Craftsmen Training in the trade of ...., this merit certificate is awarded.

महानिदेशक
Director General
रोज़गार और प्रशिक्षण/संयुक्त सचिव, भारत सरकार
Employment & Training Secretary to the Govt. of India

नई दिल्ली, ... 20
New Delhi, the 20

Appendix XXIII

Certificate of Merit for the Best State

क्र. सं. बी. एस./05
S. No. B.S./05

000009
संख्या
No.

भारत सरकार
GOVERNMENT OF INDIA

श्रम एवं रोजगार मंत्रालय
MINISTRY OF LABOUR AND EMPLOYMENT

रोज़गार और प्रशिक्षण महानिदेशालय
Directorate General of Employment And Training

अखिल भारतीय कोशल प्रतियोगिता
ALL INDIA SKILL COMPETITION

शिल्पकार प्रशिक्षण योजना के अन्तर्गत
UNDER CRAFTSMEN TRAINING SCHEME

सर्वोत्तम राज्य
BEST STATE

रनिंग शील्ड़ विजेता
WINNER OF RUNNING SHIELD

श्रेष्ठता प्रमाण–पत्र
CERTIFICATE OF MERIT

प्रमाणित किया जाता है कि .... राज्य जिसके प्रशिक्षणार्थियों में .... 20 .... में हुई अखिल भारतीय कौशल प्रतियोगिता में सभी व्यवसायों में अधिकतम कुल अंक प्राप्त किए, को योजना के अन्तर्गत सर्वोत्तम राज्य निर्णीत किया जाता है और यह दक्षता प्रमाण–पत्र राज्य रनिंग शील्ड़ प्रदान की जाती है।

This is to certify that .... state whose trainees secured the highest total marks in all the trades in the All India Skill Competition held in .... 20 .... is adjudged as the Best State under the scheme and is awarded this Certificate of Merit and the Running Shield.

महानिदेशक
Director General

रोजगार और प्रशिक्षण/संयुक्त सचिव, भारत सरकार
Employment & Training Secretary to the Govt. of India

नई दिल्ली, ... 20
New Delhi, the 20